I0803920

"If you are looking for a book that helps you to understand the lies we say to ourselves through addiction, a book that will also show you the way back and help you walk in the freedom of the gospel of Christ, you should get *Overcoming Addiction*. Read it, walk in what it says, and be helped by the clear process Brad has assembled. It will help you experience freedom, victory, and peace."

**Kike Torres,** Lead Pastor, Horizonte Cristo es Mejor, QRO, Mexico; certified biblical counselor; author

"This is spot on! It has been a true blessing to use these sound biblical principles that help people on their lifelong journey to sobriety. I became sober, by God's grace, more than fifteen years ago when introduced to *Overcoming Addiction*, and having now facilitated classes with this material for over six years, I have watched it change many lives. Excellent resource!"

**Jerry Moore, Jr,** G4-Overcoming Addictions Leader, 21 Sober

"In this book and the accompanying videos, Brad Hambrick serves as a guide who will understand your hesitations, anticipate your questions, be very clear about directions, show you the right path when you are lost, be respectful, and always have in view the God of life and love. This is a very wise and trustworthy roadmap."

**Edward T. Welch,** Faculty and counselor, Christian Counseling & Educational Foundation (CCEF); author of *Crossroads: A Step-by-Step Guide Away from Addiction* and *Someone I Know Is Grieving*

"Brad Hambrick has produced a resource that will be of such great help to those struggling with addiction. It has so many strengths—it is biblical, honest, insightful, and so very, very usable. Those who find themselves ensnared need powerful tools to break free, and this is definitely such a tool."

**Steve Midgley,** Executive Director, Biblical Counselling UK

"Insight is necessary for change, but insight without practice guarantees everything will stay the same. Few books manage to thread the necessary connection between insight and practice, tending to emphasize one or the other. *Overcoming Addiction* manages to cover both beautifully by providing a gospel-saturated, clinically sound model for addressing addictions within the context of community."

**Andrew Dealy,** Executive Director, Austin Stone Counseling Center; Director of Soul Care, Austin Stone Community Church

"Brad is excellent at noticing how the specific patterns of addiction contradict the purpose of life described in Scripture. He gives simple direction on a range of topics, including understanding motives, overcoming temptation, navigating relationships, and developing personal goals. We've used this material in support groups for years and cannot commend it highly enough in this newly published format."

**David and Krista Dunham,** Biblical counselors, Sparrow & Heart Soul Care; coauthors of *Table for Two: Biblical Counsel for Eating Disorders*

# OVERCOMING ADDICTION

# OVERCOMING ADDICTION

## 9 STEPS TOWARD FREEDOM

Brad Hambrick

New Growth Press
newgrowthpress.com

New Growth Press, Greensboro, NC 27401
newgrowthpress.com


Cover Design: Faceout Books, faceoutstudio.com
Interior Typesetting and E-book: Lisa Parnell, lparnellbookservices.com

ISBN 978-1-64507-429-8 (Print)
ISBN 978-1-64507-430-4 (eBook)

Library of Congress Cataloging-in-Publication Data
Names: Hambrick, Brad, 1977– author.
Title: Overcoming addiction : 9 steps toward freedom / Brad Hambrick.
Description: Greensboro, NC : New Growth Press, [2024] |
Series: Church-based counseling
Identifiers: LCCN 2023051647 (print) | LCCN 2023051648 (ebook) |
ISBN 9781645074298 (paperback) | ISBN 9781645074304 (ebook)
Subjects: LCSH: Addicts—Psychology. | Addicts—Rehabilitation. |
Addicts—Religious life.
Classification: LCC RC564 .H353 2024 (print) | LCC RC564 (ebook) |
DDC 362.29—dc23/eng/20240325
LC record available at https://lccn.loc.gov/2023051647
LC ebook record available at https://lccn.loc.gov/2023051648

Printed in the United States of America

31 30 29 28 27 26 25 24 2 3 4 5 6

# Contents

What Is G4? 1
The 9 Steps of G4 3
How to Use a G4 Series Book 5

**Step 1. Sometimes I Want to Be Free . . . Sometimes I Don't 8**
**ADMIT I have a struggle I cannot overcome without God.**
- Part One: Gauging My Motivation and Commitment to Change 9
- Part Two: Am I Really Addicted? 15
- Part Three: Addiction and Deceit—Two Sides of the Same Coin 27

**Step 2. I'm Afraid I Can't Handle the Truth 34**
**ACKNOWLEDGE the breadth and impact of my addiction.**
- Part One: Acknowledging the History of My Addiction 35
- Part Two: Acknowledging the Impact of My Addiction on Me 41
- Part Three: Acknowledging the Impact of My Addiction on Others 52

**Step 3. I Can't Solve the Riddle That Is Me 60**
**UNDERSTAND the origin, motive, and history of my addiction.**
- Part One: A Relational and Motivational History of My Addiction 61
- Part Two: Identifying and Talking to My Motives 68

**Step 4. Returning to God as Refuge from Substance as Escape 78**
**REPENT TO GOD for how my addiction replaced and misrepresented him.**
- Part One: To Whom Are You Repenting? 79
- Part Two: What Is Repentance? 88

**Step 5. The Courage of Honesty in the Pursuit of Sobriety** .......... **94**
CONFESS TO THOSE AFFECTED for harm done and seek to make amends.
- Part One: Expanding Your Support Network .......... 95
- Part Two: What Is Confession and How Do I Do It? .......... 101
- Part Three: Guidance for Making Amends .......... 111

**Step 6. Establishing a Satisfying Sober Life** .......... **116**
RESTRUCTURE MY LIFE to rely on God's grace and Word to transform my life.
- Part One: Removing Temptation .......... 117
- Part Two: Responding to Unavoidable Temptation .......... 124
- Part Three: Strengthening Your Body and Mind .......... 131
- Part Four: Identifying Forms of Healthy Fun .......... 137
- Part Five: Strengthening Your Soul .......... 142

**Step 7. Learning to Enjoy Living Free** .......... **147**
IMPLEMENT the new structure pervasively with humility and flexibility.
- Part One: Responding to Relapse .......... 148
- Part Two: Measuring Multidimensional Progress .......... 154
- Part Three: Assessing Life Holistically .......... 160

**Step 8. Embracing Sobriety as "The Good Life"** .......... **171**
PERSEVERE in the new life and identity to which God has called me.
- Part One: Common Lies and Distractions to Persevering .......... 172
- Part Two: How Progress in Recovery Changes Temptation .......... 179
- Part Three: Preparing for Transition from G4 .......... 184

**Step 9. Living Free to Enjoy the Life God Intended** .......... **190**
STEWARD all of my life for God's glory.
- Part One: Nine Questions to Steward Your Life for God's Glory .......... 191

**Appendix A: A Word to G4 Group Leaders** .......... **196**

**Appendix B: How to Conduct an Effective Intervention** .......... **199**

**Notes** .......... **210**

# What Is G4?

G4 is a peer support and recovery group ministry (i.e., like AA or Celebrate Recovery) built on two 9-step models that allow individuals to invest a season of their life to overcoming a life-dominating struggle of sin or suffering. G4 provides a safe environment where members learn insights and skills that will allow them to engage in biblical community more fully.

## WHY THE NAME "G4"?

**"G"** is for gospel-centered groups. Rather than making an issue, struggle, or sin the centerpiece of our groups, we strive to make the gospel of Christ the core of all our groups. *Our identity is not found in an issue but in an individual—the person of Christ.*

**"4"** designates the four types of groups that will be featured:

1. **Recovery:** Groups for those struggling with a life-dominating sin, addiction, or traumatic life event
2. **Support:** Groups for those needing encouragement and support during a period of suffering or hardship
3. **Therapeutic Educational:** Groups for those needing information and/or resources about a specific life issue
4. **Process:** Groups for those needing help processing problematic emotions or multiple life stressors

## 7 CORE VALUES OF A G4 GROUP

G4 seeks to uphold seven core values which help the ministry—both leaders and participants—care for and honor one another as they seek wholeness and holiness in their area of life struggle.

1. Bible-based and gospel-centered
2. Recognize the difference between sin and suffering
3. Built on honesty and transparency
4. Uphold confidentiality
5. Avoid struggle-based identity
6. Blend discipleship, accountability, and a guided process
7. Transitions into larger small group ministry

## SUBJECT-SPECIFIC CURRICULUM AVAILABLE

G4 has ten subject-specific curricula available. Each uses one of the 9-step models, either sin or suffering, to walk through a process for finding wholeness and holiness for that life struggle.

## SIN/RESPONSIBILITY–BASED CURRICULUM

1. False Love (sexual addiction and adultery)—bradhambrick.com/falselove
2. Gaining a Healthy Relationship with Food—bradhambrick.com/healthy
3. Overcoming Anger—bradhambrick.com/anger
4. Substance Abuse—bradhambrick.com/addiction
5. Anxiety/Depression*—bradhambrick.com/anxiety

## SUFFERING-BASED CURRICULUM

1. Anxiety/Depression—bradhambrick.com/depression
2. Navigating Destructive Relationships—bradhambrick.com/destructive
3. Taking the Journey of Grief with Hope—bradhambrick.com/grief
4. Trauma—bradhambrick.com/trauma
5. True Betrayal (processing a spouse's sexual addiction or adultery)—bradhambrick.com/truebetrayal

---

* Depression-Anxiety are dealt with together so that each can be addressed from both a responsibility and suffering paradigm.

# The 9 Steps of G4

G4 does not believe there is a one-size-fits-all solution to the struggles of life. Neither do we believe there is any magic in these sets of 9 steps. However, *we do believe that these steps capture the major movements of the gospel in the life of an individual.* We also believe that it is through the gospel that God transforms lives as he gives us a new heart.

In G4 groups, we attempt to walk through the gospel in slow motion with a concentrated focus upon particular life-dominating struggles. *We do this in a setting of transparent community because we believe God changes people in relationships.*

We believe that the gospel speaks to both **sin** (things we do wrong) and **suffering** (painful experiences for which we are not responsible) to bring *forgiveness, comfort, and hope.* We also believe that every person is both a sinner and a sufferer. However, we believe the gospel is best understood and applied when we consider how the gospel relates to the nature of our struggle. The 9 steps below are those used by G4 groups to address struggles of sin and suffering:

| SIN-BASED GROUPS | SUFFERING-BASED GROUPS |
|---|---|
| STEP 1.<br>ADMIT I have a struggle I cannot overcome without God. | STEP 1.<br>PREPARE yourself physically, emotionally, and spiritually to face your suffering. |
| STEP 2.<br>ACKNOWLEDGE the breadth and impact of my sin. | STEP 2.<br>ACKNOWLEDGE the specific history and realness of my suffering. |
| STEP 3.<br>UNDERSTAND the origin, motive, and history of my sin. | STEP 3.<br>UNDERSTAND the impact of my suffering. |

| **SIN-BASED GROUPS** | **SUFFERING-BASED GROUPS** |
|---|---|
| STEP 4.<br>REPENT TO GOD for how my sin replaced and misrepresented him. | STEP 4.<br>LEARN MY SUFFERING STORY which I use to make sense of my experience. |
| STEP 5.<br>CONFESS TO THOSE AFFECTED for harm done and seek to make amends. | STEP 5.<br>MOURN the wrongness of what happened and receive God's comfort. |
| STEP 6.<br>RESTRUCTURE MY LIFE to rely on God's grace and Word to transform my life. | STEP 6.<br>LEARN MY GOSPEL STORY by which God gives meaning to my experience. |
| STEP 7.<br>IMPLEMENT the new structure pervasively with humility and flexibility. | STEP 7.<br>IDENTIFY GOALS that allow me to combat the impact of my suffering. |
| STEP 8.<br>PERSEVERE in the new life and identity to which God has called me. | STEP 8.<br>PERSEVERE in the new life and identity to which God has called me. |
| STEP 9.<br>STEWARD all of my life for God's glory. | STEP 9.<br>STEWARD all of my life for God's glory. |

# How to Use a G4 Series Book

Thank you for picking up a G4 resource. Books in the G4 series are a bit different from most books. Most books seek to *educate you on a subject*. By contrast, books in the G4 series seek to help you *navigate a journey through a life struggle*. With most books, if you understand the content, you are ready to move to the next chapter. But in the G4 series, the goal is implementation more than education. You need to have "completed" a step, not just have "understood" its content.

For this reason, it is recommended that you work through this material with the help of others. The most common way that people work through this material is in G4 group, a lay-led counseling group hosted at a local church. You could also work through this material with a counselor or friend who is serving as a mentor. But because G4 materials take you through some of the hardest challenges in life, we strongly encourage you to enlist support as you traverse these pages.

G4 series books are the kind of literature you want to read with a pen, notebook, and Bible close at hand. This book will ask you many questions—the kind of questions that only you know the answer to, and the kind of questions that require reflection to answer. Take your time. The more honest you are, the more this book will benefit you.

This book also contains frequent devotionals that invite you to reflect on passages of Scripture. As you work through this book, we want to cultivate the habit of daily Bible study to help you find hope, direction, and meaning. Keep this book with your Bible and expect to move back and forth between the two as you read.

Often our hardships tempt us to rush, both mentally and emotionally. That means you may initially get anxious or frustrated as you work through this material. That's normal. Slowing down to reflect is difficult when life is messy. But it's worth it. Be honest about any impatience that emerges on this journey. Outside of the Bible, the best tool for change is simple honesty with people who care about you.

If you are not familiar with the 9 steps of G4, it is recommended that you review all the steps before you begin. Get the big picture of why this journey is laid out the way it is before you start working through the details of your struggle. You can find a 15-minute video that overviews these 9 steps at the following:

- bradhambrick.com/g4sin for our sin/responsibility-based curriculum. These steps are used when a life struggle emerges from our choices, beliefs, and values.
- bradhambrick.com/g4suffering for our suffering-based curriculum. These steps are used when a life struggle emerges from something we have little or no control over.
- The *Overcoming Addiction* book is built around the 9 steps for sin/responsibility–based struggles.

Too often we engage material like this in the voice of our fears and failures. As we read, we process each paragraph hearing our own self-doubt, the rejection of those we've failed, or the tone of those who have berated us for failing. This is especially true when life is hard. That is why we teach each part of each step in a free video at **bradhambrick.com/addiction**. Watching these videos before you begin each step will help you to engage this material in the redemptive tone in which it was written. Allow these videos to offset the tendency to see things through the lens of fears and failures and instead to enhance your learning experience as you take this journey.

With G4 resources, we encourage you to use the following consistent cycle to maximize your growth:

1. WATCH the video—use your phone's camera to scan the QR code to hear the step in a redemptive tone.
2. READ the step—read the material to gain a clearer understanding of what you need to achieve in this step.
3. WORK the step—do the exercises and Bible studies to make and reinforce the desired progress.

4. DISCUSS the step—share what you're learning and how you're growing with a G4 group to learn from others' experiences and how they navigated challenges like your own.
5. CELEBRATE progress—celebrate the progress you made and receive encouragement when progress is slow or you experience setbacks.
6. ADVANCE to the next step—move forward *after* you complete each step and surrender more of your life to God.

The graphic below is meant to provide a visual for this cycle. Most steps are broken into parts, so it is easier (not easy) to make consistent progress on your G4 journey. It is recommended that you use this cycle for each part of each step.

**Figure 1. The Process of Working Through a G4 Curriculum**

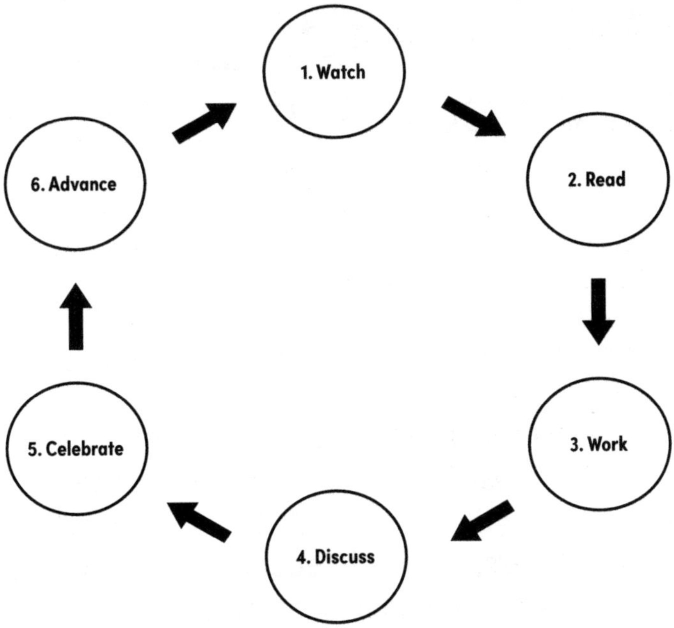


G4 series workbooks take the pace of Aesop's tortoise rather than the rabbit. Keep this in mind: be content with progress and don't get impatient with your pace. Your goal is to finish the race. Consistent progress is the best way to ensure this happens and that the change you achieve is lasting. A journey of this significance is worth the time you invest to ensure you complete it well.

# Sometimes I Want to Be Free . . . Sometimes I Don't

## STEP 1

ADMIT I have a struggle I cannot overcome without God.

At the end of this step, I want to be able to say . . .

**"Staying in my addiction and accompanying patterns of deceit would be more costly than anything God would take me through in the pursuit of his freedom. God is good for bringing me to this point of admitting my bondage."**

# STEP 1

## PART ONE

### GAUGING MY MOTIVATION AND COMMITMENT TO CHANGE

The video for this part of Step 1 can be found at: bradhambrick.com/addiction1p1.

Thank you for demonstrating courage and humility in your willingness to begin this journey. Doubtless, if alcohol or drugs have impacted your life in a significant way, many people have tried to force you to change and admit there's a problem. It is hard to embrace that change as your choice when people try to force it upon you.

That is why it is important for you to know that *every decision in this study is yours to make or not make.* Like it or not, for better or worse, the direction of your life is in your hands. This study will not attempt to compel you to do things you don't want to do.

You will be asked to honestly examine the role and impact of alcohol or drugs in your life. If it has become enslaving for you and/or harmful to those you love, you will be encouraged to pursue freedom daily through humble, honest reliance on God, with the support of those at G4. That is our encouragement to you, but that choice is yours.

This study is merely a guide. It does *not* purport superiority over 12-step groups, residential treatment, medical interventions, or your personal plan of sobriety.* Actually, this study may be used in conjunction with any of these. What you hold is a resource on finding freedom from addiction that is rooted in Scripture and supplemented with leading resources on substance abuse.

---

* In some addiction material, terms like *sober*, *sobriety*, *recovery*, *recovered*, *abstinence*, and *freedom* are debated and contrasted. In the G4 curriculum, they are used as synonyms. Early in your journey, debating these terms is usually little more than a distraction. Later in your journey, you may find these debates less important than you do now.

An initial caution is in order. Don't make a premature commitment that you're "going to do it this time." You will be asked for a formal commitment at the end of Step 2. Between now and then, we'll focus on assessing whether change is *needed* and *worth it* to you. If your answer is yes at that point, then make a commitment to change and stick with it through whatever challenges and relapses may arise. For now, a willingness to consider change is sufficient.

► **Reflection:*** What would you be giving up if you quit your addiction? This is an important and often neglected question.

> If addicts really believed that there were no positives to the addictive behavior and only negatives, they would be acting irrationally to continue to engage in the behavior. . . . An accurate evaluation of what role the behavior plays in the life of the addict appears to be an important element in fostering serious consideration of change. —Carlo DiClemente on a neglected aspect of overcoming addiction[1]

Be honest about this question. You may not like what you write. You might be ashamed to let someone else read it. Or you may really like what you write and be offended that no one understands it. *But if you are going to seriously consider changing, then you need to assess (a) what you will be sacrificing for freedom and (b) what needs to be replaced to maintain sobriety.*

> I woke up and knew I couldn't take another drink. But I also knew I couldn't live without one! —John Baker[2]

**Recommendation:** If your struggle involves drugs or alcohol, get a physical exam from your primary care physician. They can help you understand the potential withdrawal symptoms, ways to deal with those symptoms, and the nutritional deficits that may have emerged from your use. This is important for two reasons: (1) assessing the

---

* It is recommended that you keep a notebook or journal with this book. *Overcoming Addiction* is not a book you just read. To be effective you will need to study, reflect, journal, and discuss what you are learning. Give this journey the time it needs. Allow it to become a memoir of how you regained your life by the grace of God. Writing out answers to the reflections and Bible studies will also help you participate more effectively in your G4 group meetings.

toll substance abuse has taken on your body is an important factor to weigh in determining whether to commit to sobriety, and (2) if you choose to pursue sobriety, understanding these factors will allow you to create a better plan for this pursuit.

## ASSESSING YOUR LEVEL OF MOTIVATION

The pattern of changing any unwanted but enjoyable behavior is captured in the following sentiment: "Quitting smoking is easy. I've done it a couple dozen times." We want to change, but we don't want to change. We're motivated, but we're not motivated. We think we should change but wish people would just leave us alone. This mindset is called *ambivalence*—feeling two contradictory emotions about the same thing. We're good at ambivalence, even if we didn't know what it was called.

The only people you can lie to are yourself and those who love you.

- **Read James 1:5–8.** We often see these verses as just a guilt passage. We read it and think, *If this applies to me, I should freak out. God must be mad at me.* Start with verse 5 and realize the passage begins by presenting God as generous. *God is not upset about supplying what we need in our double-minded moments.* This will help us trust that there is hope for our fickle desire to change (v. 6). God won't change us against our will. That we won't receive anything from God as long as we are double-minded also means God refrains from imposing himself on us (v. 7). Instead, he is loving and warns us against the dangers of our double-minded tendency. *At this stage in your journey, you're just starting to get comfortable admitting what God already knows.* There is hope because God is not surprised even if we are surprised when we admit how bad things have gotten. Hope begins where you are, and God will always join you there.

You need to name this tendency toward ambivalence early in your journey. Don't feel ashamed of your conflicted motives. God already knows about them, and he still wants to help. *The only people you can lie to are yourself and those who love you.* In this section, you will look at Carlo DiClemente's five stages of motivation to change from his book *Addictions and Change*: **pre-contemplation**, **contemplation**, **preparation**, **action**, and **maintenance**. I've included in parentheses how these stages correlate with the 9-step journey of this study, as well as my own summary of each stage below:

1. **Pre-Contemplation** (before you started G4): This is the stage when you didn't anticipate making any changes because you didn't think change was needed. You were probably offended if someone suggested that you needed to change.

2. **Contemplation** (Step 1): Now you are beginning to believe that change might be beneficial and are wondering what the process might look like. You are trying to decide whether change is possible, and, if so, if it's worth it. You want to know what would be required and whether these sacrifices would produce a more satisfying life than continuing in addiction.

3. **Preparation** (Steps 2–4): In this phase you embrace the reality that change is needed. You gather the information necessary to enact an effective and sustainable plan. You assess obstacles, both logistical (external) and motivational (internal). You begin to enlist people to come alongside you for the journey.

4. **Action** (Steps 5–7): At this point plans come to life; ideas become choices. Progress is made and you navigate setbacks. There are successes and failures, but the trajectory of your journey is forward. Techniques become habits and habits become a lifestyle. The roles once filled by your addiction are now filled with healthier, God-honoring ways of managing life.

5. **Maintenance** (Steps 8–9): You embrace a new lifestyle. Increasingly your emotions and thought patterns conform to this new lifestyle. Your addiction is no longer your reward or escape of choice so you are enjoying life. At this stage you begin the work of restoring relationships and pursuing interests that were damaged or made impossible by the addiction.

Although I've presented these stages as corresponding to the 9 steps of G4, stages of motivation are not linear. It's common for people to jump between stages during their journey out of addiction. For example, you may feel strong motivation to change on Monday (action) but fall on Friday and wonder if the journey is even worth it (contemplation). The goal is not to move in a straight line from one stage to the next, but to realize that no matter where you are in the process, the Lord is there and able to help you.

> There is no shame in falling; only quitting.

- **Exercise:** In the margin beside these five stages of motivation, write "*today*" beside where your motivation is now. Write in the margin *significant dates or events* that came to mind when you read each description. This may not be your first attempt at this journey. But you can learn something beneficial from every partially successful attempt you've made. *There is no shame in falling; only quitting*. It's also important to recognize when you begin to cover new terrain in your journey.

If you struggle with addiction to multiple substances or behaviors, you may not be in the same place—motivationally speaking—with each one of them. Be honest about that too so that you can weigh the implications of tackling your addictions one at a time versus all at once.

In the chart below, list the addictive substances and activities you might struggle with in the first column. Then for each one, place an "x" under the stage of change that best represents where you are.

- If you doubt there's a problem, mark "pre-contemplation."
- If you're willing to consider whether this item represents an addiction, mark "contemplation."
- If you're committed to change and are actively creating a plan, mark "preparation."
- If you are actively working on recovery in this area, mark "action."
- If you are working to preserve more than six months of sobriety in this area, mark "maintenance." There is no magic in reaching the six-month mark. The indication of six months here is merely meant to be a minimum mark before considering your growth to have reach a maintenance phase.

| Substance/ Activity | Pre-Contemplation | Contemplation | Preparation | Action | Maintenance |
|---|---|---|---|---|---|
| | | | | | |
| | | | | | |
| | | | | | |
| | | | | | |

Your goal at this point is to become more self-aware of your motivation to change. You want to be aware when your motivation fluctuates. It will. Growth in awareness allows you to grow in honesty with others. Honesty with self, God, and others is foundational to change. Everything at G4 is built around this honesty.

## G4 GROUP DISCUSSION: STEP 1, PART ONE

As you discuss this material in G4 group, these questions are meant to facilitate a more honest and beneficial dialogue about this material. Anyone is free to respond to whichever questions they choose.

### Experienced Members

- What do you remember about the pre-contemplation and contemplation phases of your journey?
- What factors or experiences were influential in your choice to embrace the pursuit of change?

### New Members

- What brings you to G4? How much of your story are you willing to share?
- What about your addiction do you most dread giving up?
- How can we pray for you?

### Everyone

- What mental or emotional habits indicate you're regressing to a pre-contemplation phase?
- If you could talk to yourself in your "John Baker–quote moments," what would you say?
- Have you experienced a significant setback or victory since last meeting that you should tell the group?

# STEP 1

## PART TWO

### AM I REALLY ADDICTED?

The video for this part of Step 1 can be found at: bradhambrick.com/addiction1p2.

The primary virtue required to complete Step 1 is courage—the courage to engage with questions and challenges we've developed ingrained habits to avoid. If you feel a reflex to retreat as you work through this material, be honest about it. Courage doesn't mean the absence of internal resistance. Courage means we're honest about the internal resistance we feel and we continue toward our goal in spite of that resistance.

In this part of Step 1, you are going to be asked to consider what you've long debated. The question is, "Do you have an addictive relationship with drugs or alcohol?" Many people have likely tried to convince you that the answer is yes. As much as possible, we would like you to engage this question objectively. Try to resist allowing defensiveness from previous conversations to bias your answers. Thank you for your courage as you try to do this as accurately as possible.

## ADDICTION ASSESSMENT

**Instructions:** Read the following descriptive statements. Mark the answer that most accurately describes your behaviors when they were at their worst *in the last three months*. If you struggle with multiple addictions, either complete a separate assessment for each addiction or answer according to whichever addictive behavior is most intense for that criterion.

**(N) almost never, (R) rarely, (S) sometimes, (F) frequently, or (A) almost always**

For the most accurate results, ask one person who is aware of your addictive behaviors from each major sphere of your life (i.e., home, work, social, church small group, etc.) to complete this assessment on your behalf and compare results. If you choose to enlist others, you must be willing to hear their perspective without arguing or debating. One sphere does not negate another. For instance, a good report from a friend does not mean your spouse is inaccurate about your actions.

In this assessment **AoD stands for "alcohol or drugs"** and can also include tobacco products, legal medications not used according to prescription, or behaviors known to be personally or relationally destructive.

| | |
|---|---|
| 1. I have used AoD to a degree that impaired my judgment or self-control. | **N R S F A** |
| 2. When using AoD I have embarrassed myself or damaged my reputation. | **N R S F A** |
| 3. I have been a poor steward of my time due to my consumption of AoD. | **N R S F A** |
| 4. I take pride in how much I can drink or use without being impaired. | **N R S F A** |
| 5. The type and amount of AoD I've used has exceeded what I meant to consume. | **N R S F A** |
| 6. I have used alcohol underage, prescription meds for nonmedical purposes, or illegal drugs. | **N R S F A** |
| 7. I have been significantly impaired or have passed out while using AoD. | **N R S F A** |
| 8. I sometimes feel guilty after using AoD. | **N R S F A** |
| 9. I have hurt or offended loved ones and friends while using AoD. | **N R S F A** |
| 10. What I see as right, wrong, or permissible has changed since I began using AoD. | **N R S F A** |
| 11. My conscience, before I began using AoD, would be offended by how I use them now. | **N R S F A** |
| 12. I am more defensive than I was before I began using AoD. | **N R S F A** |

| | |
|---|---|
| 13. I am beginning to plan my week around acquiring and consuming AoD. | **N R S F A** |
| 14. I use AoD to manage unpleasant emotions. | **N R S F A** |
| 15. I would feel cheated if someone around me had AoD and I did not participate. | **N R S F A** |
| 16. The rhythm of my week would change significantly if I didn't use AoD. | **N R S F A** |
| 17. When I know someone doesn't drink or use drugs, I doubt we could be friends. | **N R S F A** |
| 18. I consider whether I will have the funds necessary for AoD when making financial decisions. | **N R S F A** |
| 19. I have a strong association between mundane activities (i.e., meals, places, moods) and AoD. | **N R S F A** |
| 20. I lie about my consumption of AoD. | **N R S F A** |
| 21. I have noticed that it takes more AoD to have the same effect. | **N R S F A** |
| 22. AoD no longer have the "new high" feel I remember at first. | **N R S F A** |
| 23. I spend more time and money consuming AoD than I did initially. | **N R S F A** |
| 24. I buy higher proof alcohol or more potent drugs than I did initially. | **N R S F A** |
| 25. I have learned to manage hangovers better than I did initially. | **N R S F A** |
| 26. I don't feel "normal" without AoD. | **N R S F A** |
| 27. I have anxiety, restlessness, irritability, headaches, or a lack of concentration without AoD. | **N R S F A** |
| 28. I experience sweating, muscle tension, chest tightness, tremors, or nausea without AoD. | **N R S F A** |
| 29. My family and friends find me less pleasant to be around without AoD. | **N R S F A** |
| 30. I know that quitting AoD would be a physical challenge for me. | **N R S F A** |
| 31. I begin to crave AoD when I have not had them for a while. | **N R S F A** |

| | |
|---|---|
| 32. I find it harder to manage my emotions or difficult situations without AoD. | **N R S F A** |
| 33. AoD are one of my top rewards when I have done something good. | **N R S F A** |
| 34. I feel punished when I don't have AoD. | **N R S F A** |
| 35. My desire for AoD is stronger than my desire for things like food or friends. | **N R S F A** |
| 36. AoD have strained my relationship with family and friends. I am more isolated. | **N R S F A** |
| 37. I have chosen to continue using AoD even when it has cost me friends. | **N R S F A** |
| 38. The quality of relationship I have with my children is less because of AoD. | **N R S F A** |
| 39. Family and/or friends have confronted me about my need to stop using AoD. | **N R S F A** |
| 40. My use of AoD has resulted in a negative performance evaluation or job loss. | **N R S F A** |
| 41. I have experienced a change in my weight because of AoD. | **N R S F A** |
| 42. I have sustained an injury while using AoD. | **N R S F A** |
| 43. My immune system is weaker because of AoD (i.e., I get sick frequently). | **N R S F A** |
| 44. I experience constipation, irritable bowel, or appetite changes because of my AoD use. | **N R S F A** |
| 45. I am forgetting or losing more things because of my AoD use. | **N R S F A** |
| 46. I have been arrested (or could have been) because of my AoD use. | **N R S F A** |
| 47. My actions while using AoD have resulted in life-threatening events. | **N R S F A** |
| 48. I lost custody of my children (even temporarily) or lost other rights because of AoD. | **N R S F A** |
| 49. I have legal issues due to my AoD use. | **N R S F A** |
| 50. Even in the face of negative consequences, I feel life is better with AoD than without. | N R S F A |

**Scoring Key:** Each criterion is assessed with five questions and should be scored as indicated below:

- "N" and "R" response = 0 points
- "S" response = 1 point
- "F" response = 2 points
- "A" response = 3 points
- If your total score is 5 to 9, it is a significant concern.
- If your total score is 10 or higher, it is a life-dominating struggle.

The material for this assessment is organized into three categories, which are often referenced in addiction research, although different counselors use different vocabulary. Understanding these categories will help you apply what you learned from this assessment. Let's now take a closer look at the stages and the specific questions from the assessment.

| Stage of Addiction | Common Addiction Language | Craig Nakken's Language in *The Addictive Personality*[1] | Ed Welch's Language in *Addictions: A Banquet in the Grave*[2] | Questions |
|---|---|---|---|---|
| Stage One | Use | Internal Change | Sin | 1–15 |
| Stage Two | Abuse | Lifestyle Change | Slavery | 16–35 |
| Stage Three | Dependence | Life Breakdown | Tragedy | 36–50 |

**Stage One—Use/Internal Change/Sin:** Addiction begins with unwise or immoral experimentation. *We must cross lines of folly and sin to reach the level of addiction. To reclaim sobriety, we must retrace our steps back across these lines.* These are simple principles which are profoundly challenging for at least two reasons. First, sin is not just something we do (behaviors) but our innate inclination from birth (we are born with a sin nature). Second, as an addiction develops, the practice becomes more instinctual than volitional and, therefore, has a greater grip on our life.

- Questions 1–5: (Total: _____ in 5 questions)

  These questions describe a **violation of wisdom principles**. Even if your potentially addictive behavior is morally and legally permissible, it must cross over the line of wisdom into folly for it to become a controlling presence in your life. For this reason, as you go through this study, you will examine in greater detail how you were willing to make unwise choices. Wisdom will be one of your greatest friends in the pursuit of sobriety (Proverbs 1:20–33). *Take comfort in the fact that wisdom is pursuing you even when you are not pursuing it.*

- Questions 6–10: (Total: _____ in 5 questions)

These questions describe a **violation of moral precepts**. For addictive behavior to gain control in our lives we must also cross moral lines into sin. This happens in two ways: First, *we begin to rely on our addiction for things that only God can provide* (i.e., comfort, strength, courage, etc.). Second, *we rely on our addiction to resolve problems created by our addiction.* For instance, we may fail to love our neighbor as ourselves because of our addictive behavior. When they get upset with us because of this failure, we reengage our addiction to escape the stress.

> To become permanent, addiction must make itself at home in the rhythms of your life.

- Questions 11–15: (Total: _____ in 5 questions)

These questions describe a **fading of conscience and willpower**. An addiction gains control by callousing our conscience and weakening our will (Ephesians 4:19). *We enter a new phase of danger when we no longer experience our increasingly addictive behavior as destructive and no longer have the desire to forsake it.* Our will and conscience must be rekindled if we hope to fight the addiction or even acknowledge the need to do so.

**Stage Two—Abuse/Lifestyle Change/Slavery:** We often will not admit the presence of an addiction until we begin to reap its most severe consequences (Stage 3). But there is a phase when the will and conscience have not been completely seared and life is not yet falling apart. This phase has the *logistical marker* of a lifestyle forming around our addiction, *physiological markers* of tolerance and withdrawal, and the *psychological marker* of craving.

- Questions 16–20: (Total: _____ in 5 questions)

These questions describe our **lifestyle forming around addiction**. To become permanent, addiction must make itself at home in the rhythms of your life. Identifying and countering these lifestyle adaptations are essential parts of developing an effective and sustainable plan for overcoming addiction. Therefore, more attention will be given to understanding these changes in subsequent parts of this study.

> It takes choice and commitment to continue to obtain effective access and to seek the addictive behavior when negative personal and social consequences begin to emerge. . . . The addicted individual appears to be functioning more on autopilot than choosing. Nevertheless, a chosen commitment to the addictive behavior continues. . . . There are virtually hundreds of little decisions that are made daily and weekly to ensure access to the behavior. Arranging schedules, making excuses, sneaking off for periods of time, and minimizing consequences are all part of the process of protecting continued engagement in the addiction. —Carlo DiClemente[3]

- Questions 21–25: (Total: _____ in 5 questions)

These questions describe **tolerance**. Our bodies were made by God to be remarkably adaptive. As you engage your addiction, your body creates a "new normal" to accommodate this new substance or practice. For instance, as you drink alcohol, your body adapts by producing more alcohol metabolizing enzymes. The result is (a) your body becomes more efficient at processing alcohol, and (b) it takes more alcohol to reach intoxication.

- Questions 26–30: (Total: _____ in 5 questions)

These questions describe **withdrawal**. Tolerance leads to withdrawal. If tolerance means your body is adapting to a "new normal," then withdrawal is your body's response to the absence of this "new normal." For this reason, withdrawal symptoms tend to be the opposite of the pleasurable effects of your AoD of choice. For example, withdrawing from stimulants leaves you feeling lethargic, or withdrawing from pain medications results in you feeling achy (in excess of whatever pain you may have been trying to medicate).

- Questions 31–35: (Total: _____ in 5 questions)

  These questions describe **psychological dependence/craving**. Even for substances and activities that do not create tolerance and withdrawal, psychological dependence can still emerge and become enslaving. Addictions alter the reward center of the brain and thereby our motivational systems. This is why we can experience controlling cravings even when the biological phenomena of tolerance and withdrawal are not occurring. This is also why addiction cannot be reduced to mere biology and neurology.

**Stage Three—Dependence/Life Breakdown/Tragedy:** When we surrender control to a substance or activity, life falls apart. Sin, the predatory evil present in and around our lives, seeks our demise (1 Peter 5:8). This is why we believe addictions are also spiritual struggles. Addiction is the epitome of our flesh ruling over God's Spirit in our lives (Galatians 5:16–24). *In addiction and recovery, we see the contrast between our enemy's destructive reign and God's benevolent reign over our lives (John 10:10–11).* Sobriety is about both the absence of a particular behavior and the presence of a new allegiance in our life.

- Questions 36–40: (Total: _____ in 5 questions)

  These questions describe **relational and professional damage**. Addiction is as relational as it is behavioral; it is about who and what we value as much as what we do. For this reason, some of addiction's most profound destruction will occur in our closest relationships.
- Questions 41–45: (Total: _____ in 5 questions)

  These questions describe **damage to our health**. While our bodies are incredibly adaptive (see tolerance), this adaptation does not avert damaging health effects. The changes in our body created by addiction leave us in a living state that is increasingly distant from God's design for a healthy human body. The sooner you are willing to acknowledge these changes, the more their impact can be averted or countered.
- Questions 46–50: (Total: _____ in 5 questions)

  These questions describe **tragic life consequences**. The ability of addiction to destroy our lives goes beyond our relationships and bodies. Financial ruin and legal consequences are only two of many examples that could be given. As with anything in the "Tragedy—Stage 3" level of the addictive process, if you are not currently experiencing these effects, do not allow this to become a "things aren't that bad" excuse. If you are at Stage 2, then allow these Stage 3 criteria to be a warning instead of a tool for minimization and denial.

## EXAMINING NINE DEFINITIONS OF ADDICTION

It is hard to talk about addiction without debating definitions. "What is an addiction? Is it a disease or a choice? Does it reveal a character deficit or a pitiable condition?" You've probably heard these debates and may have strong opinions about the best answers. We want to communicate in this curriculum that if we frame the definition of addiction in a binary, either-or fashion, we are likely to leave out an important part of the conversation.

> Sobriety is about both the absence of a particular behavior and the presence of a new allegiance in our life.

Hopefully, you can already pick up that this study will draw some from both schools of thought. *Every addict makes choices, and addiction radically changes how we choose.* The path out of addiction is lined with the stepping stones of meaningful choices, and we are all predisposed (by our fallen, sinful nature) to resist these choices. The more we make unhealthy choices, the stronger our propensity for destructive choices becomes.

**Caution:** Do not get bogged down in this section. This material will make more sense in retrospect, with a bit more sobriety under your belt. But the debates surrounding this subject are too prevalent to leave unaddressed until the end of our journey.

Nine definitions of addiction are provided below from the resources frequently referenced in this study. Proponents of each definition believe their description offers a valuable perspective on the experience of addiction. This is not the time to try to write the perfect definition of addiction or deconstruct the philosophical assumptions behind each. At this point, look for something beneficial in each definition.

1. "Addiction is bondage to the rule of a substance, activity, or state of mind, which then *becomes the center of life, defending itself from the truth* so that even bad consequences don't bring repentance, and leading to further estrangement from God." —Ed Welch[4]
2. "The critical dimensions for an addiction are (1) the development of a solidly established, problematic pattern of an appetitive—that is, pleasurably reinforcing—behavior, (2) the presence of physiological and psychological components of the behavior pattern that create dependence, and (3) the interaction of these components in the life of the individual that make behavior resistant to change." —Carlo DiClemente[5]
3. "Addiction is any compulsive, habitual behavior that limits the freedom of human desire . . . *When we can see our freedom impaired, we should consider the presence of addiction.*" —Gerald May[6]
4. "Addiction is a pathological love and trust relationship with an object or event." —Craig Nakken[7]
5. "Addiction is an impulse-control disorder." —Craig Nakken[8]
6. "The language of sin that AA rejected was not the orthodox doctrine of sin as propounded by thinkers like Augustine. Rather, AA rejected a certain understanding of sin [Pelagianism] that had long been found theologically wanting. The church proclaims that sin is not fundamentally about human acts but about the human situation. The acts that we call sins are derivative of a deeper malaise called sin." —Kent Dunnington[9]
7. "They become conscious of the fact that they have been merely fighting the symptoms of *some deep-seated malady*, and that they are confronted, not merely with the problem of sins, that is, of separate sinful deeds, but with the much greater and deeper problem of sin, of *an evil that is inherent in human nature* . . . Sin does not reside in any one faculty of the soul, but in the heart, which in Scriptural psychology is the central organ of the soul, out of which are the issues of life. And from this center its influence and operations spread to the intellect, the will, the affections, in short, to the entire man, including his body." —Louis Berkhof[10]

8. "The thematic has thus come full circle. What was originally understood as the universal condition of sin, then reduced to the pathology of a particular group, and then expanded into a proliferation of addictive diagnoses has simply become another name for a universal human condition." —Linda Mercadante[11]
9. Summary (Brad's definition): *Addiction is present whenever continued self-destructive behavior is chosen over healthy living that honors God and those we love.*

As you reflect on these definitions, ask yourself two sets of questions:

1. **What did you learn that was helpful?** Put these things in your own words. Personalize them. Own them. What are the things that feel true, but you're prone to bristle toward? Put these things in your own words too. Acknowledge your resistance to them and begin to let your heart thaw toward them.
2. **What important misconceptions are challenged?** What did you discover that you needed to unlearn? Where did you find yourself thinking, *I wish my family or friends understood this?* The best opportunity to clarify these misconceptions happens on the other side of your sobriety. Persevere in your journey. Your progress will help establish your credibility to speak into how the church and your community understand addiction. But remember, your recovery is the first step.

## G4 GROUP DISCUSSION: STEP ONE, PART TWO

As you discuss this material in G4 group, these questions are meant to facilitate a more honest and beneficial dialogue about this material. Anyone is free to respond to whichever questions they choose.

### Experienced Members

- What things do you remember feeling "really important" at this phase in your journey that, looking back, were more of a distraction than beneficial?
- Which phrases or concepts in the definitions of addiction were most beneficial on your journey?

New Members

- Which questions in the addiction assessment were most difficult for you to answer objectively?
- What did you learn about yourself and the experience of addiction from completing the assessment?
- How can we pray for you?

Everyone

- What is your biggest internal obstacle to admitting where you are on your recovery journey?
- In what areas of your life have you been tempted to regress back toward thinking "continued self-destructive behavior seems easier and more appealing than healthy living"?
- Have you experienced a significant setback or victory since last meeting that you should tell the group?

# STEP 1
## PART THREE

### ADDICTION AND DECEIT—TWO SIDES OF THE SAME COIN

The video for this part of Step 1 can be found at: bradhambrick.com/addiction1p3.

If this entire journey could be reduced to a single step, it would be this—*be honest.* Honesty may be more difficult than sobriety. At the risk of being offensive, you can't be a good addict without being a good liar. You won't get far enough into the process if you can't cover your tracks. Once you're in the addiction, the lies you've told become the bars in your personal prison. Honesty is the number one "technique" to emancipate yourself from addiction.

The most dangerous lies are the ones you believe. The first person with whom you need to be honest is yourself. When you believe your own lies, they become more convincing to others and cripple the motivation necessary to change.

> When lies become your native language, you are in trouble. . . . The more lies you've told . . . the more lies you believe. —Ed Welch[1]

> We are as sick as our secrets. . . . Remember it is always better to tell the ugly truth rather than a beautiful lie. . . . Truth often hurts. But it's the lie that leaves the scars. —John Baker[2]

Memorize this statement—*you will never be more free than you are honest.*

- **Read Numbers 32:23; Proverbs 15:3; Job 34:21; Luke 8:17; and Hebrews 4:13.** You may have already experienced the truth contained in these verses. We lie because we believe we can control the truth by the stories we tell and the information we give or withhold. We begin to believe we are larger than the truth, rather than believing that truth is the reality in which we live. We can no more control truth than we can control the wind. *Remind yourself regularly that honesty is not optional; the only thing we can choose is if and when we are honest.* Truth will be known. Pause and pray again for the courage to be honest, because truth-speaking and sobriety are also two sides of the same coin.

> Honesty is the number one "technique" to emancipate yourself from addiction.

In many ways, this section may be the hardest part of this entire journey. It will be hard for at least two reasons. First, it will require you to disarm the primary mechanism of protection for your addiction. Second, it will require you to be honest with yourself about *how* you've been dishonest; not just *what* you've misrepresented.

One way to think of the deception involved in addiction is *fragmentation* (telling parts or fragments of your story as if they were the whole story and expecting others to respond accordingly). This is what we do when we ask a friend for financial help, they respond that we need to address our addiction, and we respond, "I thought you were my friend and that I should ask my friends for help when I face hard times. I guess I was wrong." We take two fragments (i.e., friendship and hardship) and expect our friend to respond as if this were the whole story. When they point to other pieces of the story (i.e., the number of times we've borrowed money and not repaid before), we get offended.

## ADDICTION: 10 WAYS WE DECEIVE OTHERS

1. **Omitted facts.** The story you tell is true and there are no false statements in it. However, the most relevant information for maintaining sobriety is omitted. For example: Saying "I went to the store and picked up a few things. Here's the milk you said we needed," but failing to mention the six-pack you bought with cash on a separate receipt.

   *As a rule, if there is a question you hope is not asked, then you should voluntarily disclose the answer.* People should not have to ask the right question to get the needed information to help. That is the equivalent of a patient lying to their doctor about where it hurts because he didn't specifically ask, "Are you having chest pains?"

How do you lie by omitted facts, and what are the most recent or significant examples?

2. **False facts.** This is a step beyond omitting facts. The story may be true, but elements of the story are false. For example, saying "I got to talk to my sponsor today, and he said he was really encouraged by how things were going," but your sponsor called because he was concerned about your lack of recent contact.

   *If anything you say is false, then everything you've said is self-destructive.* We never lie to cover up the things that make our life better. We only lie when what we've done is offensive to others or destructive to ourselves.

   How do you lie by false facts, and what are the most recent or significant examples?

3. **False emotion.** Now you must play the part. If your lies are true, then they would require certain emotions. If you are going to remain "free," then you must become an actor. When we feign emotions to protect our addiction, the "audience" does not know they're watching a "show." This makes our deception even more destructive to the relationship because now our loved one realized that not just our words—but also our emotions—were a performance.

   *Lying by false emotions is the best way to teach people to mistrust you.* When people doubt both our words and emotions, they lose faith in anything we say, unless they see direct evidence.

   How do you lie by false emotions, and what are the most recent or significant examples?

4. **False story.** False facts produce false emotions. Together they require a false story. Your lies begin to create their own world in which they could be true. You try to live between reality and your false story. Reality won't bend, and your lies can't break without you being found out. You and those around you are forced to live stretched between these two worlds.

Telling the truth now means more than correcting facts. Initially, this form of lying feels the most powerful because you're playing a godlike role. *Acknowledging this type of lying is the most shameful because we realize how much we have manipulated everyone around us.*

How do you lie by false story, and what are the most recent or significant examples?

5. **Minimizing.** Maybe you are smart enough to avoid the false route. Maybe you can see how that would inevitably blow up in your face. Instead, you choose the "better" route. You don't change the facts, but merely change the significance of those facts. Minimizing is one of the more popular methods of lying.

   *You should not weigh any addictive behavior until it's been fully disclosed to someone acquainted with your struggle.* The significance of drinking two beers is different when you're in addiction than when you haven't been. Find someone who is committed to your sobriety and who knows you well. They can help you determine the severity of a setback. Avoid language that sizes a concern as small: "slip," "mishap," "mistake," etc.

   How do you lie by minimizing, and what are the most recent or significant examples? What phrases do you use to minimize?

6. **Blame-shifting.** Maybe you accept the facts and admit how serious the problem is, but you lie by shifting the responsibility. "It's true and it's bad, but it's not my fault." Some of the favorite targets for blame-shifting are your spouse, your friends, your history, your personality, your emotions, or "it just happened." *Engaging your addictive behavior is always a choice.* Focusing on anything other than the influence of your choices to use your substance of choice puts your sobriety in jeopardy.

   As a rule, explanation comes after ownership. If you are trying to explain why something happened or remedy the influences that contributed to the setback before fully owning your choices, you are blame-shifting.

   How do you lie by blame-shifting, and what are the most recent or significant examples? Who or what are your favorite targets for blame-shifting?

7. **"I don't know."** It is legal to "plead the fifth" in a courtroom, but it is deceitful in recovery. "I don't know" is often used to buy time while preparing to do a "better" job at one of the other forms of lying. *"I don't know" is also used to force the questioner to nag or badger so their action can become the focal point of the conversation.*

   If you know the answer but are not proud of it, share it anyway. If you are tempted to blame-shift, be honest about it—"Right now I'm having a hard time answering your question because I can tell I'm wanting to blame others." If you are genuinely uncertain, answer as clearly as you can and acknowledge the incompleteness of your answer—"I know this won't completely answer the question you've asked, but here is what I can explain about my actions . . ."

   How do you lie by "I don't know," and what are the most recent or significant examples?

8. **Late truth.** Post-discovery confession is not honesty. Often, we want points for admitting what people already know. When we add the false emotion of being offended that "our best is not good enough" or "I'll never be able to please you," we only compound the situation.

   *Expecting trust by merely acknowledging truth that had already been discovered is manipulative.* It is like expecting to be paid for someone else's work. Remember, you only earn trust for truth that you voluntarily contribute to the relationship.

   How do you lie by late truth, and what are the most recent or significant examples?

9. **Changing definitions.** Altering the definition of words is one of the most prevalent tactics of manipulation. How many times has someone said, "I thought you were my *friend*" to assuage a situation where their addiction was being put on the spot? Here "friend" is being defined as "someone who wouldn't give me a hard time about living in a self-destructive manner." *Forgiveness* and *trust* are two other words frequently distorted during manipulative-addictive conversations.

   *Be very cautious when you are hinging your defense or a request on an emotionally loaded word like "friend," "forgiveness," or "trust."* There is a strong probability you are using these words, intentionally or not, in a manipulative manner.

How do you lie by changing definitions, and what are the most recent or significant examples?

10. **Exaggeration.** This is deception by magnification. Unlike other forms of lying, which seek to shrink or hide the truth, exaggeration makes the truth larger than it really is. Truth moves from being an enemy to being a weapon. For example, using words like *always*, *never*, and *only*.

    Exaggeration places the emphasis on your perspective or experience more than truth. Exaggeration is an attempt to force people to live in your world rather than join them in the real world. Addiction creates a proclivity for all-or-nothing thinking. *Learning to live between minimizing and exaggerating is both the essence of honesty and the remedy for the all-or-nothing thinking of addiction.*

    How do you lie by exaggeration, and what are the most recent or significant examples?

> In addiction, as in all of life, we overcomplicate things in order to avoid facing the truth. —Gerald May[3]

## FINAL THOUGHTS ON STEP 1

Now is a pivotal time in your process of change. If you remain alone in your pursuit of sobriety, you will likely fail. The most important thing you can do at this point is to involve someone else (preferably multiple people) in your pursuit of God's freedom from addiction. This is why this curriculum is written to be studied in a G4 group. You need the support and examples that come from walking alongside people on a comparable journey.[4]

> Do this work with someone else. Addictions are private, so doing this in public is a way to take a stand against your addiction. —Ed Welch[5]

To reach the end of this first step is a significant achievement. Well done! It is difficult to wrestle through the number of subjects you've already addressed and to face things you've tried to avoid for some time. Honor the work you have put in to reach this point by continuing to take the next steps toward freedom.

> There I humbly offered myself to God, as I then understood Him, to do with me as He would. I placed myself unreservedly under His care and direction. I admitted for the first time that of myself I am nothing; that without Him I was lost. I ruthlessly faced my sins and became willing to have my new-found Friend take them away, root and branch. I have not had a drink since. —Bill Wilson, founder of Alcoholics Anonymous[6]

## G4 GROUP DISCUSSION: STEP 1, PART THREE

As you discuss this material in G4 group, these questions are meant to facilitate a more honest and beneficial dialogue about this material. Anyone is free to respond to whichever questions they choose.

> If you remain alone in your pursuit of sobriety, you will likely fail.

### Experienced Members

- What was hardest to admit in your pattern of deceit?
- When you began to get serious about recovery, how self-aware were you when you were deceiving?

### New Members

- How hard is it for you to hear, "You can't be a good addict without being a good liar"?
- What patterns of deceit are you most prone to use?
- How can we pray for you?

### Everyone

- What has been the clearest example of your being self-deceived about the severity of your addiction?
- Can you echo the final quote from Bill Wilson as being representative of where you are?
- Have you experienced a significant setback or victory since last meeting that you should tell the group?

## I'm Afraid I Can't Handle the Truth

---

# STEP 2

## ACKNOWLEDGE the breadth and impact of my addiction.

---

At the end of this step, I want to be able to say . . .

**"I am beginning to see the extent and impact of my addiction. It is bigger than I wanted to admit [describe your minimization] and still may be bigger than I realize. Apart from God's grace, I would continue to be a person in bondage. I acknowledge that there is no hope and no freedom in minimizing my addiction. Before I can truly understand the significance of Jesus in my life, I must acknowledge the magnitude of what he is empowering me to overcome."**

# STEP 2

## PART ONE

### ACKNOWLEDGING THE HISTORY OF MY ADDICTION

The video for this part of Step 2 can be found at: bradhambrick.com/addiction2p1.

Thank you for continuing this journey. It takes courage to persevere in something this difficult. You are to be commended for completing Step 1 and beginning Step 2. In this step we will examine the breadth and impact of our addictions. In Step 1, we named our struggle; now we will examine it.

Metaphorically speaking, in Step 1 we said, "I have a dog." In Step 2 we will assess whether we have a poodle, Labrador, or Great Dane. There is an important advance in this second step. We can admit a problem exists while still minimizing its severity. The reality is that *our level of commitment and efforts toward change will correspond with how severe we believe our addiction is*. If we underestimate the problem, we are unlikely to persevere through the process of change.

> Every time you decide on an important change, you are choosing your future.

With that in mind, as you progress through this step, resist the urge to get defensive or overwhelmed. This step is merely about rightly naming reality. Acknowledging is hard work. Because we've denied and minimized the problem, it feels like life is getting worse when we acknowledge the breadth and impact of our addiction. But that is not true. Life is not getting harder; our vision is just getting clearer.

As you begin Step 2, begin with this thought experiment. Be as honest and objective as you can.

- ▸ **Reflection:** What do you think will be the result if you continue with your addiction(s) for the next 5–10 years?

Every time you decide on an important change, you are choosing your future. Step 2 is about preparing you to make a more informed choice. This takes courage. In the short-term, it would be emotionally easier to ignore the things we will examine. But choosing to transition from pursuing short-term relief to pursuing long-term benefit is key in overcoming addiction.

At the end of this step, you will be asked to decide, *"Is change worth the effort?"* The following pages will help you (a) answer this question wisely and, if you decide yes, (b) have the information needed to continue on this journey effectively.

## THE HISTORY AND GROWTH OF MY ADDICTION

Think about a rainbow; not a bold-color-contrast rainbow like those in a children's book, but a real rainbow in the sky. Can you tell the exact point at which red ends and orange begins? How about the point where blue quits being blue and becomes violet? On a spectrum, transitions are hard to define, but key distinctions are not. In the middle of each stripe, it is easy to discern blue from green.

The movement from use, to abuse, to dependence is like this as well. But unfortunately, we often use this ambiguity in these transitions to deny that blue has become green; that use has become abuse, or abuse has become dependence. The purpose of this section is not to pinpoint moments where these transitions occurred. They did not likely happen in moments. Instead, we want to look back and own (that is, take non-self-deprecating responsibility for) the reality that these transitions have occurred.

We are not going to retrace our steps out of addiction; undoing each thing we did to get where we are. The only way out of addiction is forward. We can't unwrite history, but we can learn from it. We can practice being more honest with our self, God, and others by how we tell our story. We can practice being fully known and learn to grapple with whatever unpleasant emotions emerge from that.

- **Exercise:** Write your answers to these questions. This will take some time and reflection. You will do more writing than reading in the first part of Step 2. You don't have to write in great detail. You are not writing an autobiography. You are outlining enough that you can (a) be honest with your G4 group and supportive friends/family, and (b) have a history to review as you identify wise steps forward.

- When did you *start* using? Be specific for each substance of abuse.
- When did you *stop* being honest? Be specific about how dishonesty emerged in each circle of relationships.
- When did the pain you were *avoiding* become more satisfying than the high you were *gaining*?
- When did being sober begin to feel *less normal* than being high or intoxicated?
- At how many junctures did your addiction change who your *friends* were? When did it start feeling like it would be hard to be friends with people who did not share your addictive behavior? How did your view of people who didn't share your addiction begin to change to support your addiction (e.g., "They're naive," "They think they're better than I am," "They don't know how to have fun")?

> We can't unwrite history, but we can learn from it.

- What rituals or *daily routines* have built up around your substance of choice usage? Another way to ask this is, how would your rhythms have to change if your substance of choice was not a part of your life?
- When did you begin to feel a *sense of shame* about the things you were neglecting to pursue due to your addiction?
- What key events alerted you that things had gotten worse than you intended them to?
- Make a list of the *drinking rules* you have made for yourself. When did each rule emerge? What was each rule meant to disprove or control? How did each new rule "move the line" for a previous rule?

  Drinkers, for example, have their own definition of the amount or pattern of drinking they consider to be out of control. If the individual's drinking does not meet this definition, he or she believes that it is under control.

> Such definitions might include drinking before noon; drinking hard liquor instead of beer (because beer is not considered strong alcohol); and drinking alone instead of at bars because there is moderation in numbers. —Carlo DiClemente[1]

It's just as important to remember the successes you want to build on as it is to assess the failures you want to overcome. With every incomplete effort at ending our addiction, we can learn important things about what change will require. Resist the urge to feel ashamed or hopeless because of failed attempts at ending your addiction. Learn from them. In that vein, consider these questions as well:

- Since you began to abuse your substance of choice, what are the longest periods of time you have been sober? What did you like about these times? What prompted you to think about change and made change worth it to you at those times?
- What were the most important factors that contributed to these seasons of sobriety? What things did you do that helped you avoid your substance of choice? What things did you remove from your life that helped you avoid your substance of choice?
- What relationships or interests that you enjoyed began to emerge or reemerge during these seasons of sobriety?
- What are the skills and interests you have which could flourish if they weren't crowded out by your substance of choice? If you could invest the time and energy that you currently give to addiction to something else, what would you want that something else to be?

► **Read Matthew 10:4; Mark 3:18; Luke 6:15; and Acts 1:13.** As we see in these passages, one of Jesus's disciples was known as Simon the Zealot. This meant he had been part of a violent group that sought to overthrow or undermine the government. In our day, Simon's pre-conversion occupation would have been called terrorism or extremism. The frequency with which he is referenced as "Simon the Zealot" in Scripture indicates that he learned to tell his story without shame or pride. That is the ultimate goal of this section. It won't be completed in this step. But as you tell the story of how God changes your life, it should be marked by decreasing amounts of shame (hiding details you wish were not true) and pride (using the severity of your struggle to discredit the ability of others to speak into your life).

Ultimately, Simon took on a different identity—both personally and socially. He began to be known as one of the twelve disciples. This also captures two goals that we hope you will embrace in your journey. First, Simon changes from having a hardened, individualistic approach to life to finding joy in belonging to a group. We hope you find that sense of belonging in your G4 group and a local church. Second, Simon's old identity rooted in his sin of choice was overshadowed by his new identity as a follower of Christ. His old lifestyle was referenced only to highlight what was possible in his new identity. It was an invitation to others (i.e., change is possible) rather than a mark of shame.

Putting the work into telling your story accurately is an important part of this kind of transformation in your own life.

## G4 GROUP DISCUSSION: STEP TWO, PART ONE

As you discuss this material in G4 group, these questions are meant to facilitate a more honest and beneficial dialogue about this material. Anyone is free to respond to whichever questions they choose.

### Experienced Members

- How has the way you remember the development of your addiction changed during your time in G4?
- What was the most important part of how you thought about the development of your addiction that needed to change for you to make progress in recovery?

### New Members

- Which of the history of addiction questions was hardest for you to answer? Do you mind telling us a little about the internal obstacles you faced as you tried to be honest about it?
- What parts of your daily routine are most important to change for you to continue in recovery?
- How can we pray for you?

**Everyone**

- What drinking or using rules did you use to convince yourself or others that you didn't have a problem?
- How does the devotion on Simon the Zealot help you acknowledge the presence of addiction without embracing the shame of feeling like you'll always be known as an addict?
- Have you experienced a significant setback or victory since last meeting that you should tell the group?

# STEP 2

## PART TWO

### ACKNOWLEDGING THE IMPACT OF MY ADDICTION ON ME

The video for this part of Step 2 can be found at: bradhambrick.com/addiction2p2.

Our choices change us. Every choice we make either builds us up or tears us down; every choice adds to or detracts from our flourishing. In this part of Step 2, you will examine how your addiction negatively impacted your life. You will examine four ways that drugs and alcohol impact your life.

1. Effects on our physical body
2. Effects on our mind and emotions
3. Effects on our identity
4. Effects on our daily, functional living

You are studying this material to do a comparative analysis. You are seeking to answer a big question: "Is change worth it?" As you note the changes you have already experienced and the costs of continuing in your addiction, you are creating a tally. You are tabulating the impact of your addiction to compare it to the effort required to change. The goal of G4 is to help you make an honest, informed choice that sets you up to "love God and love others" well (Matthew 22:37–40).

### PHYSICAL EFFECTS

Whenever the negative health effects related to your substance of choice are discussed, the inevitable counter is to discuss the positive health effects. Both can be true. When both positive and negative health effects exist for the same substance, their impact is represented by a bell curve; the initial benefits peak with moderate use and then quickly slide into significant health concerns. When moderation is lost, health will be compromised.

> In any event, all data agree that the consumption of three drinks per day offers no benefits over those observed with one or two, and at four drinks per day the risk for heart disease and cancers as well as other life-threatening problems increases significantly. —Marc Schuckit[1]

However, this brings up an important dynamic in the discussion of addiction. Most of us had strong warnings against our substance of choice as children. These warnings included education about the dangers of our substance of choice. When we experimented but these dangers did not occur, we assumed the warnings were false exaggerations intended to scare us. *The pleasures* of your substance of choice *are quick, episodic, and intense. The dangers* of your substance of choice *are delayed, cumulative, and lasting. This combination of factors allows for a high degree of self-deception.* Avoid the mistake of dismissing the warning signs we're learning about in Step 2; the deterioration of your health, damage to relationships, and other life consequences. Heed these warning signs about where you are in the progression of your addiction rather than waiting for them to get worse.

- **Read Genesis 3:1–24.** What was one of Satan's primary strategies in tempting Eve? He called into question long-term consequences that had not had the time to come to fruition, "You will not surely die" (v. 4). God never said, "You will drop dead on the spot" but that death would be an inevitable conclusion to life. Eve, like us with our warnings about addiction, could say, "The warning didn't prove true." *Satan was deceptively accurate in the short-term and deadly wrong in the long-term.* He used this strategy to cause Eve to doubt God. *Satan still uses this strategy to get you to doubt parents, teachers, friends, or any other voice that would lead you to the way of life.* Be aware of Satan's empty sales pitch so you can begin to doubt it.

In this section we will examine ten body organs and systems affected by addiction. These effects take time so we often doubt their inevitability when they take a few years or decades to develop. But because addiction abuses our body, some combination of these is bound to occur.

1. **Kidneys.** Your kidneys filter your blood. Therefore, the more foreign substances you put in your body (by quantity and potency), the harder your kidneys must work. Your kidneys literally lay down their life to protect the rest of your body by storing these substances until they can be metabolized and removed.

2. **Liver.** The liver plays a filtering function like the kidneys. The negative effect of drugs on the liver can range from general symptoms (e.g., fatigue, nausea, and loss of appetite) to more severe symptoms (e.g., jaundice, enlarged liver, pain in the upper right abdomen, confusion, disorientation, and reduced alertness).

3. **Heart.** Most illegal drugs can have adverse cardiovascular effects, ranging from an abnormal heart rate to heart attacks. Injecting illegal drugs can also lead to cardiovascular problems such as collapsed veins and bacterial infections of the blood vessels and heart valves. Any change in your body's energy level will affect the activity level of your heart. The more you artificially change your heart rate, the unhealthier it is for your heart.

4. **Lungs.** Next to the brain, drugs impact the lungs more than any other organ. Even when drugs are not consumed through smoking, drugs interact with the gas exchange that happens in our lungs, making it more difficult for our lung tissue to exchange gases. The damage to delicate lung tissue is exemplified when the drugs are smoked.

5. **Immune system.** When the body is under stress of any kind, one of the first places it pulls energy from is the immune system. Irregular sleep patterns, imbalanced nutrition, and other body stressors created by abuse of your substance of choice further decrease the amount of energy the body can devote to the immune system.

6. **Digestive system.** Anything you put in your mouth that burns (e.g., liquor), burns all the way down. Opioid drug use can lead to constipation. After your body adapts to abusing these, the result is a season of irritable bowel. When our body adapts to the unhealthy circumstances we force upon it, the result is pain and suffering.

7. **Exposure to Diseases.** In addition to a suppressed immune system, abusing your substance of choice frequently leads to increased exposure to diseases. Habits of personal hygiene are neglected. Compromises in judgment result in more risky health behaviors (i.e., unprotected sex, sharing needles, etc.).

> Bring your pain to God—even when you caused it.

8. **Dental problems.** The side effects of many drugs include dry mouth or teeth grinding due to increased energy levels and body tension. Both side effects result in significant tooth decay.

9. **Hormones.** The body has biological priorities, and testosterone for men or estrogen for women are not at the top of the list. When the body is under a degree of stress, it neglects functions unrelated to survival. So, in the same way the immune system is neglected during stress, so is the production of a variety of hormones. The impact on your health varies based on which hormone is suppressed, but the effects are significant.

10. **Brain.** In the next section, we will examine the cognitive and emotional changes that addiction produces, but here we will consider the physiological changes that happen in the brain. Addictions interfere with neurotransmitters, damage connections within the brain, and reduce the ability to experience pleasure. These physical changes account for many of the difficulties in breaking free from an addiction.

The more parts of our body that become uncomfortable, the more prone we become to abuse our substance of choice. We begin to use more of our substance of choice to offset the very symptoms our drug of choice created.

> No matter how they start, addictions eventually center in distress and in the self-defeating choice of an agent to relieve the distress. In fact, trying to cure distress with the same thing that causes it is typically the mechanism that closes the trap on an addict. —Cornelius Plantinga, Jr.[2]

▸ **Read Psalm 102.** We do not know if the affliction experienced by the author of this psalm had anything to do with addiction. But, regardless, we find in this psalm an invitation to make our physical pain known to God. Notice the rise and fall of this psalm. It doesn't move smoothly from despair to hope. It has many ups and downs. But even its downs are Godward downs. *This is the pattern God wants you to follow.* Bring your pain to God—even when you caused it. God is willing to comfort you in your suffering even when it's caused by your sin—sin that he is eager to forgive if you are willing to relinquish it.

## EMOTIONAL-COGNITIVE EFFECTS

Often, we falsely assume our brain only has one control center. In reality, our brain has three. *Emotion, reason, and reward have their own region of the brain where they weigh incoming data and arrive at conclusions.* An imperfect metaphor would be that these control centers are like the three branches of the United States government and meant to hold each other in check.

One way to understand addiction is that reward and emotion mutiny against reason. Taken too far, this metaphor reveals why many addicts believe they will never be able to live sober: *if reason has to dominate over reward and emotion, then the only way for me to be sober is to never be happy*. But the actual goal is a balance of power, not a reverse mutiny. Restoring balance may feel like suppressing reward and emotion initially, but recovery is merely restoring balance to these three faculties.

Let's consider eight possible emotional-cognitive effects of addiction. As you read, ask yourself, "Which of these do I experience?

When? How does my substance of choice and addictive lifestyle contribute to these?"

1. **Depression.** There are at least three ways addiction can contribute to depression. First, many of our substances of choice are depressants. It only makes sense that consuming significant quantities of a depressant would increase your level of depression. Second, it is physically exhausting to be addicted. Fatigue increases the rate of depression. Last, addiction requires time, and this time comes at the expense of rewarding activities.

2. **Anxiety.** Stimulants are to anxiety what depressants are to depression. Additionally, the mounting number of daily chores and work-school responsibilities that are neglected because of addiction create a growing sense of anxiety. It is often this sense of being overwhelmed that causes us to retreat again to processing life through our emotion and reward centers.

3. **Shame.** The emotion of shame is a strong indicator that our addiction is seeping into identity. One common way to differentiate guilt and shame is that guilt is a negative emotional response to *what we've done* while shame is a negative emotional response to *who we are.*

4. **All-or-nothing thinking.** This may be the most destructive cognitive disruption that emerges because of addiction. In this mode of thinking, things are either great or awful, easy or impossible, perfect or ruined, etc. Since overcoming addiction is a journey and requires a process, it feels impossible.

5. **Distorted sense of time.** Addictions work fast. A "delayed onset addictive substance" is an oxymoron. If there was a cheap drug that had a long high but a twenty-four-hour delay between consumption and its effects, it would not be popular. The low cost and pleasurable high would not offset its delayed effect. This accounts for how addiction begins to dominate life. *Most things worth doing take time. When addiction creates a life built around immediacy, we lose our tolerance for these*

*long-term investments. This also undermines recovery because recovery takes time.*

6. **Negative emotion intolerance.** The goal of addiction is to feel good or at least not to feel bad. The more we build our life around this value, the less we are able (or willing) to tolerate unpleasant emotions. Empathy, uncertainty, grief, boredom, insecurity, doubt, and similar emotions become reasons to use. The more we escape these normal, unpleasant emotions through substance use, the more intolerable we perceive them to be.

   A primary effect of a distorted sense of time and negative emotion intolerance is impulsivity. As we increase our demand for immediacy and lose tolerance for anything unpleasant, our decision-making becomes profoundly reactionary. We are no longer thinking. We begin to simply demand and escape.

> Remembering that addiction is not your identity is an important part of not surrendering your power of choice.

7. **Paranoia.** There are at least two factors related to addiction that can foster paranoia. First, addiction involves regularly violating our conscience, at least the part that remains sensitive (1 Timothy 4:2), and sometimes involves violating the law. These factors create a growing sense that we are doing something wrong and that everyone knows it. Second, AoD can deteriorate the prefrontal cortex of the brain. The result is that we struggle to discern rational fear from irrational fear, which fuels paranoia.

8. **Inflated sense of normal.** After the prolonged exposure to the artificial reality created by our substance of choice, normal feels dull, painful, muted, or subdued. It is comparable to the experience we have after jumping on a trampoline. When we are off the trampoline, our normal jumping feels stunted.

► **Read Psalm 51.** Notice that David prays that God would "restore to me the joy of [my] salvation" (v. 12). He was aware that his sin with Bathsheba (the artificial high of an illicit relationship and high stakes political maneuvering to cover it up) had impacted his thinking and emotions. He needed them to be recalibrated. The purpose of this section is to raise our awareness of what we are asking God to restore so that we can increasingly cooperate with God's grace through faith and obedience.

## IDENTITY CHANGE

The longer we do something, the more it becomes part of who we are. Addictions, by definition, are prolonged behaviors. Therefore, addictions tend to have a profound impact on our identity. *With addictions, we not only invest a significant amount of time and money, but we also sacrifice many dreams and relationships to feed our addiction. These dynamics only increase the degree to which our addiction becomes part of our identity.*

> In fact, the longer we struggle with a problem, the more likely we are to define ourselves by that problem (divorced, addicted, depressed, codependent, ADD). We come to believe that our problem is who we are. But while these labels may describe particular ways we struggle as sinners in a fallen world, they are not our identity! If we allow them to define us, we will live trapped within their boundaries. This is no way for a child of God to live! —Paul Tripp[3]

Once a struggle has become who we are, we feel even more powerless to change it. Therefore, it is vital for you to remember there is a "you" who struggles with addiction. Addiction is the parasite. You are the host. It is powerful. It has home turf in our sin nature and world filled with suffering. But, by the grace of God, you (not "it") make every decision.

When addiction wins, you enact its agenda. That is not a word of condemnation, but a word of hope. You don't have to ask permission to change. You can continually surrender to a new master, Christ. But it is *you* who will make that choice every time. Remembering that addiction is not your identity is an important part of not surrendering your power of choice.

## FUNCTIONAL EFFECTS

Addictions don't exist in a vacuum. They exist in space and time. They cost money. They require planning. They force us to rearrange priorities. While addictions may be hard to define, it is easy to identify their functional effect on our life. *Addiction is not just an activity; it's an investment and a lifestyle.* When we only view addiction as recreation, it is easier to minimize it.

In this section, we will look at four functional effects of addiction. These four impacts will serve as a transition for you to consider how your addiction is affecting others (Step 2, Part Three).

1. **Time.** There are two types of time investment in addiction: direct time and indirect time. Let's first consider direct time.
    - How many hours do you spend using your substance of choice? _____ per week _____ per month
    - How many hours do you spend high or intoxicated? _____ per week _____ per month
    - How many hours do you spend "hung over"? _____ per week _____ per month

2. **Planning and covering up.** The indirect time associated with addiction has to do with planning and covering up your addictive behaviors.
    - How many hours do you spend planning for your addiction? _____ per week _____ per month
    - How many hours do you spend covering up your addiction? _____ per week _____ per month
    - How many hours do you spend ensuring access to your addiction? _____ per week _____ per month

    These first two points allow us to make a very practical assessment that has probably already crept into your thinking, "Is the amount of time I'm spending on this study 'worth it'?" Now you can do the math.

    Hours Working G4 Steps: _____ per week
    Hours in Counseling/Group: + _____ per week
    Hours Invested in Addiction: - _____ per week (total from points one and two)
    Net Gain/Loss _____ per week

This is not a math trick. It's reality. This is an example of allowing reason to have its right role over emotion and reward. *When the answer to "is sobriety worth it?" becomes an emotional decision, you make choices that cost you huge portions of your future.*

3. **Money.** Scripture calls us to consider the financial cost of addiction (Proverbs 21:17; 23:21) to awaken ourselves to the danger and folly of our actions.

   Money spent on AoD: _____ per month
   Money spent because of guilt: _____ per month
   Money lost because of work missed: _____ total
   Money lost due to injury or accident: _____ total

   Now convert this total amount of money into hours (by dividing it by your hourly wage) and include it in the "worth it" computation about your net gain in time. If you make $20 per hour and the total financial loss in this segment is $1000, then that is an additional 50 hours of your life you have spent on your addiction ($20 x 50 hours = $1000).

4. **Priorities.** This functional effect is less tangible. We can't create a countable commodity like hours or dollars. But the lack of tangibility does not make this impact less significant. The questions below are meant to help you identify the way addiction has changed your priorities.
   - What dreams have died, or have you stopped pursuing because of addiction?
   - What relationships have been lost, or at least placed at risk, because of addiction?
   - What opportunities have you not pursued because of addiction?
   - What difficulties do you willingly live with instead of abandoning your addiction?
   - What values and beliefs have you changed to accommodate your addiction?
   - What would you want better for your children than you are experiencing because of your addiction?

► **Read Romans 5:1–11.** After an examination like this, we will wrestle with shame. It is hard to acknowledge what we see in the mirror. This passage reminds us that shame need not be our destiny (v. 5). But, *if we want to experience change, we must face our shame. Jesus bore its penalty, but we cannot avoid its reality*. On this point, C. S. Lewis offers a helpful metaphor. Lewis compared shame to hot coffee. If we spill hot coffee on our skin we are burned, scalded, and feel disgusting. However, if we drink coffee we are warmed, nourished, and energized. When we avoid shame or wallow in shame, it becomes like spilled coffee. Scripture reframes our shame and allows us to draw closer to Christ in our weakness.

## G4 GROUP DISCUSSION: STEP 2, PART TWO

As you discuss this material in G4 group, these questions are meant to facilitate a more honest and beneficial dialogue about this material. Anyone is free to respond to whichever questions they choose.

### Experienced Members

- Which of these effects of addiction were you most prone to ignore early in your journey?
- How have you seen the devotion on Romans 5 play out in your life?

### New Members

- Which of these effects of addiction got your attention and helped you become willing to join G4?
- How are you managing the amount of time that recovery is giving you back?
- How can we pray for you?

### Everyone

- How has addiction impacted your sense of identity? How has working these steps improved that?
- What did you take from the devotions on Psalm 51 and 102 that was helpful?
- Have you experienced a significant setback or victory since last meeting that you should tell the group?

# STEP 2

## PART THREE

### ACKNOWLEDGING THE IMPACT OF MY ADDICTION ON OTHERS

The video for this part of Step 2 can be found at: bradhambrick.com/addiction2p3.

This part of Step 2 will take *courage.* It is why the word *fearless* is used in Step 4 of AA: "Make a searching and fearless moral inventory of ourselves." In G4's 9-step approach, this inventory is interspersed in our first three steps. What you're doing isn't easy, but it is necessary for change. If this step creates an emotional disruption that jeopardizes your progress in recovery, seek additional support from a friend, pastor, counselor, or group.

We will look at three types of impact our addiction may have had on others:

1. Active offenses
2. Absent offenses
3. Atmosphere changes

In short, we will examine what we've done to hurt others, what we've left undone that has hurt others, and the relational culture created by our addictive lifestyle—a culture in which those who love us or depend on us were involuntarily forced to live. Things we identify in this part of Step 2 will serve as the basis for seeking to make amends in Step 5.

## ACTIVE OFFENSES

Active offenses are things you did to cover up or perpetuate your addiction that harmed others. *These are things you did which made it clear that something (your addictive behavior) was more important than someone (the person you sinned against).* Regretting those choices later does not reduce their impact. Minimizing their importance, frequency, or impact only enables your addiction. Our goal is to be honest enough to facilitate our progress in recovery and healing for those we hurt.

Our goal is to be honest enough to facilitate our progress in recovery and healing for those we hurt.

- **Lies.** We have covered this in significant detail in Step 1. You cannot be a good addict without being a good liar. As your actions become more destructive you become better at covering them up to perpetuate the addiction. **To whom have you lied about your addiction or its impact?** How did you lie? If all they had was the information from you, what inaccurate or incomplete perspective do these people have?
- **Stealing.** Addictions aren't cheap, especially when they become so dominant that they impair your ability to earn money. Consider stealing in at least two forms: (a) taking money or property that is not yours, and (b) receiving pay for hours that you did not perform up to the expected standard because of your addiction. **From whom and how have you stolen to perpetuate your addiction?**
- **Character assassination.** When people won't believe our lies, we either have to tell them the truth or vilify them. Either we're wrong, or they're mean, harsh, rude, legalistic, intrusive, etc. Notice how both slander and a lack of self-control (a primary contributor to addiction) are listed in 2 Timothy 3:1–5. The Bible recognizes that if we don't own our shortcomings, we will push them off on others. **Whose character have you maligned to protect your addiction?**

► **Read Exodus 20:1–21.** These are the Ten Commandments. Too often we approach these as rules; that is, limitations on our freedom imposed on us by God. When we view the Ten Commandments this way, God seems harsh and controlling. However, we can begin to see that violating these commandments is actually what limits our freedom. Take a moment to reflect on the number of other times in life where you've confused bondage with freedom. Where have you dismissed true freedom by believing others (even God) were trying to control you?

## ABSENT OFFENSES

Christians have long held to the distinctions between sins of commission (i.e., things that we do which are wrong) and sins of omission (i.e., things that are wrong to leave undone). We can harm relationships and hurt people as much by our non-actions as we can by our actions. The time we give to addiction is time we should have used to bless others.

- **Relational withdrawal.** This refers to your absence from others. There are people who love you. They want to be with you. When you withdraw, they are rightfully hurt. Friends, parents, spouse, children, and coworkers have a fair expectation of your reasonable availability. When you withdraw, you place them in a lose-lose scenario. If they pursue you, you accuse them of nagging and being controlling. If they honor your distance, then you use this as evidence they don't care. **From whom have you created a lose-lose scenario by relationally withdrawing?**
- **Isolation.** This refers to other people's inability to access you. Metaphorically speaking, withdrawal means someone must call; isolation means you won't answer the phone. When you isolate, you force those who love you to either place their life on hold or move on without you. This is another example of how your sins of omission create a lose-lose scenario for those around you. **From whom have you isolated yourself in a way that disrupts their life?**
- **Dependability.** When you say yes to something, it is right for people to take you at your word (Matthew 5:37). There are probably many things you've said yes to because you knew they were reasonable requests, but you failed to follow through on because of your addiction. This creates a third type of lose-lose scenario. If they accommodate your lack of dependability, they are enabling your addiction. If they try to force your compliance or micromanage your involvement, then you claim this is an unfair lack of trust. **With whom have you been undependable?**

## ATMOSPHERE CHANGES

These changes are less tangible and, therefore, more easily overlooked. But less tangible does not mean less real. It just means they are harder to define. It may be harder to own these offenses at this stage in your journey, but at least begin to give them greater credence. These changes are disruptive because they become an unhealthy lifestyle we impose on those who love us. *Our children, spouses, parents, and close friends live within the new, unhealthy "normal" our addiction creates.*

- **Emotional confusion.** Imagine a parent who yells about misplaced socks, ignores failed tests, and falls into self-pity when their child runs away. In this example, the size of the parent's response does not correlate with the size of the offense. In addiction, we are like that parent. The size of our response does not correlate with the size of the event we're responding to. Those around us live in confusion because there is little correlation between the size of our reaction and the event that prompted it. **For whom have you created emotional confusion by your inconsistent reactions?**
- **Six degrees of separation.** This happens when we refuse to discuss anything remotely related to our addiction. We don't want to talk about drinking, so we don't want to talk about our plans Friday night, so we don't want to talk about any of the friends we were with, so we don't want to talk about the common interests that would make our loved one think of these friends, so . . . you get the idea. Pretty soon most of our life feels off limits. Those who love us can't figure out what they're doing wrong to get an aloof or defensive response. **Who have you trained to know the "off limit" topics with a version of the six degrees of separation game?**
- **Addiction replaces relationship.** In relationships, we can tell where we rank in other people's lives. "If I ask for [blank] and [name] asks for the same thing, who gets it?" When we struggle with addiction, those who love us get used to living with a sense that there is a "mystery other" in our lives. Even before they know about our addiction, they know they are second to someone or something. After they learn of our addiction, they begin to realize the rank of the addictive substance is

comparable to an adulterous partner in a marriage. Their sense of betrayal is real and legitimate. **Who has been replaced or demoted in your life due to your addiction?**

> Your addiction went from being a friend to a lover to a slave-master. —Ed Welch[1]

- ▸ **Read Matthew 22:37–40.** This is the well-known "Golden Rule" passage. Everything we've talked about in this part of Step 2 is a violation of the command to "love your neighbor as yourself" (v. 39). Adhering to this simple principle is sufficient to protect us from hurting those around us in the ways we've described. But it is not easy. *The opposite of simple is complex. The opposite of easy is difficult. This means things that are simple may not be easy.* Your loved ones may have said, "It seems so *simple* what needs to be done." And they're right. Basic honor in a relationship is not complex. But chances are you've heard them say, "It should be *easy* to do these things." Part of owning your addiction is the ability to say, "It is simple. What I need to change is clear and straightforward. I can admit that. But it is not easy. It is, actually, quite difficult for me. But I am committed to a process of making the changes that clearly need to be made." This kind of statement allows you to be honest without minimizing your struggle. This honesty without overpromising or becoming overconfident is a key way to begin loving your neighbors as yourself.

**Now we come to the big question: Is change worth it?** You have the information you need to make an informed choice. Now is the time to decide whether (a) you believe you need to change, and (b) whether you are willing to commit to the process of change. The time for merely gathering information and pondering options is over.

*This is the purpose of these first two steps: to help you make an informed choice about the future that you want.* Now you're being asked to make a commitment to change. Engaging the rest of this material in this journey without a firm commitment to change would be counterproductive. You would think "it didn't work" because your commitment was half-hearted.

You know change is hard, so it doesn't make sense to try to change without a firm commitment to the process. The "My Commitment to

Change" sheet on page 58 is meant to help you solidify your commitment. If your answer to "Is change worth it?" is yes, then fill out this form, make copies, and give a copy to your fellow G4 group members, sponsor, counselor, parents, spouse, and others supporting you on this journey.

Your plan will develop as you continue this study. But when you feel your sense of commitment begin to wane, do two things:

1. Reach out to the people supporting you on this journey. Do this immediately and without delay. Don't worry about what you're going to say or what it will sound like. Just make the call.
2. Review your "My Commitment to Change" sheet and your work from the initial two steps to remind yourself of why this journey is worth it.

## G4 GROUP DISCUSSION: STEP 2, PART THREE

As you discuss this material in G4 group, these questions are meant to facilitate a more honest and beneficial dialogue about this material. Anyone is free to respond to whichever questions they choose.

### Experienced Members

- Looking back, what were the atmosphere changes you now realized you forced your loved ones to live in that were hard to see when you began?
- How has being honest and available to those you love been a blessing instead of the threat you initially feared?

### New Members

- What is one thing you have been less than fully honest about since you've been in G4?
- What is your biggest remaining obstacle to fully committing to change (if any)?
- How can we pray for you?

### Everyone

- How did the contrast between simple and easy in the devotion on Matthew 22 help you face the relational challenges involved in overcoming addiction?

- What are the most tangible ways your addiction acted like an affair in your closest relationships?
- Have you experienced a significant setback or victory since last meeting that you should tell the group?

## MY COMMITMENT TO CHANGE[2]

This is your plan. The most important words on this page are *I*, *me*, and *my*. Do not allow yourself to begin to view these things as something that is being forced upon you. Write the things that are important to you and the things you believe will be effective. As you learn more about yourself through this study, you can modify your plan. But, at this stage, be sure that you are fully embracing this as *what you want for your future.*

You are ready to commit when you believe the freedom you'll gain is greater than the bondage you'll lose.

> The treatment for addiction is to want something better than your addictions. . . . Hope is the conviction that the battle is worth it. —Ed Welch[3]

> Human behavior change requires significant effort. . . . The reasons in favor of change need to be important and substantive enough to move the individual into deciding to make the effort to change. —Carlo DiClemente[4]

**The changes I want to make are:**

**The most important reasons I want to make these changes are:**

The steps I plan to take in changing are:

The ways other people can help me are:

| PERSON'S NAME | WAYS THEY CAN HELP |
|---|---|
| | |
| | |
| | |
| | |

I know that my plan is working if:

Some things that could interfere with my plan are:

I am hopeful these consequences or results will come out of my recovery change plan:

## I Can't Solve the Riddle That Is Me

# STEP 3

## UNDERSTAND the origin, motive, and history of my addiction.

At the end of this step, I want to be able to say . . .

**"I do not know all I need to know about myself or my addiction. I do know my heart resists being known (Jeremiah 17:9), and that my cravings reveal the things that are most important to me (Luke 6:45). I am coming to realize that [list specific] desires lead me to addiction, and that [list key past] experiences have contributed to the strength of those desires.**

**However,**

**I believe God is more satisfying than those desires could ever be without him,and that a life honoring God can reshape the strengths of my desires."**

# STEP 3

## PART ONE

### A RELATIONAL AND MOTIVATIONAL HISTORY OF MY ADDICTION

The video for this part of Step 3 can be found at: bradhambrick.com/addiction3p1.

We often fall into the trap of thinking that if we understand the "why" better, then the "what" will be easy, or at least easier. There are at least two realities that interrupt this seemingly sound logic.

First, sin is not rational, so it refuses to play by our rules of logic. *Sin is not a simple behavior that operates according to single-variable motivations. Rather sin is a condition and a predator.* Sin has its roots in our fallen human nature. Sin is aided and abetted by an enemy who desires our destruction (1 Peter 5:8). This means that sin both has the home field advantage and is willing to cheat to win. This is why the addiction-as-disease understanding has become popular. It recognizes that sin is more than the bad choices we make.

Second, *our goal must be effectiveness-at-change rather than ease-of-change.* Sin is always willing to wait for a more opportune time (Luke 4:13). The moments when we let our guard down are the times when our intelligent adversary will strike. Anything that decreases our vigilance is an asset to our adversary.

These realities do not make an examination of the history and motives of our addiction fruitless. It means that what we intuitively want from this examination is often overly optimistic. What we can gain is a better understanding of the following:

a. what motives drive our addiction,
b. the context in which those desires become excessively dominant, and
c. how those desires begin to take on a godlike function in our lives.

The more we can make these assessments honestly and accurately in real time, the more effectively we will be at relying on God and reaching out to our support network for help. The more foreign or crazy our motives feel to us, the less likely we are to tell others what is going on. The more these things make sense to us, even if we disagree with the values behind the motives, the more willing we will be to ask for help.

## ANOTHER LOOK AT YOUR HISTORY

In Step 2, we looked at the history of your addictive behaviors. This was helpful in seeing how the breadth and impact of your addiction grew. In Step 3, we will consider history from three new angles:

1. How your relationship with your addiction grew—*addiction slowly becomes the most important thing in your life.*
2. How your relationships impacted the development of your addiction—*family and social history impact your motives.*
3. How motives change over the history of your addiction—*motives don't remain the same and aren't simple.*

In the context of G4, this section serves two functions. First, this section allows you to grow in self-awareness. It is an opportunity for you to get to know you better. We often bewilder ourselves. The sprint and crash pace of addiction, along with the turmoil addiction creates around us, interferes with honest self-reflection.

Second, this section allows your group to get to know you better. To do this we'll need to traverse the twin dangers. First, we need to accept that each person's story is unique. We cannot dismiss support from people whose story is different from our own. We must resist thinking, *Well, if you haven't [blank], then there's nothing I can learn from you.* Second, we must avoid imposing our story on other people's story. We don't like when people say, "I know . . ." and impose their story on ours. Resist the urge to read your story onto someone else's story when a few of the details sound familiar. Honoring each other's story by listening well is a key aspect of an effective group for overcoming addiction.

Take the time to answer these questions and reflect on the implications:

- *Have members of your family struggled with addiction?* A family history of addiction both removes the taboo of addiction and provides you with a working model of how to live in addiction. Addiction feels more "normal" when it has been part of your immediate family.
- *How did your family handle emotions and conflict?* A significant part of addiction is the unhealthy attempt to regulate our emotions. The less your family handled emotion and conflict in a healthy way, the less equipped you may feel to handle life without addiction. There are skills we may have to learn and strengthen.
- *How safe was it to have weaknesses or make mistakes in your family?* The unrealistic pressure to always be strong or "on" creates an emotional climate where you feel the need for an unhealthy outlet or deception. Overcoming addiction often requires us to grow in healthy vulnerability about our weaknesses.
- *How socially competent have you felt at various stages in your life?* AoD are often used as "social lubricants," at least initially. The more we rely on a crutch like AoD, the less likely we will develop the skills to navigate social contexts without AoD.
- *When challenges come, are you predisposed to address them or ignore/escape them?* The more avoidant we are to life challenges, the more appealing substance abuse becomes as a form of escape.
- *When you were first "wowed" by your AoD of choice, what created the "wow"?* Often addiction is an attempt to get this first experience back. Be honest about this without portraying the wow as a good thing. For example, if you say, "I felt free for the first time in my life," also say, "and I realize that chemically induced freedom is an illusion."
- *When you have tried to quit before, what kind of experiences had the biggest impact on your relapses?* Relapses should always be viewed as a learning opportunity. Don't beat yourself up for past relapses. Learn from them. What kind of things tripped you up? In what stages of recovery did you become overconfident?

► **Read Romans 12:3.** This passage tells us to think of ourselves with sober judgment. *"Sober" here doesn't mean not intoxicated; it means with a realistic and accurate assessment.* This section and the remainder of Step 3 focus on this topic. Romans 12:3 acknowledges that God gives each one of us different "measures of faith." Part of this person-to-person variance are the strengths, weaknesses, and aptitudes that allow us to endure stressors and temptations. Each one of us differs in what tempts us, why certain things are tempting, and how intense a temptation may be. Paul tells us not to be ashamed of this (which only leads to more hiding and lying), but to be honest and order our life wisely according to a sober assessment of who we are.

Honoring each other's story by listening well is a key aspect of an effective group for overcoming addiction.

## EVOLVING MOTIVES ACROSS THE HISTORY OF ADDICTION

Identifying and assessing motives is not as straightforward for addiction as it can be for other life struggles. With anger or anxiety, you can ask, "Why am I angry?" or "Why am I anxious?" and once you have an answer, the steps toward resolution are relatively clear. You may need to repent of your pride, back off how much you value a pet peeve, change how you manage finances, or modify expectations in relationships. In these situations, identifying motives makes the logistics of change decently clear.

This is not the case with addictions. *The category of addiction implies enough time has passed for the addictive behavior to (a) have many motives feeding its life, and (b) have motives that have become self-perpetuating.*

> **An example of A:** A teenager may begin to drink based on peer pressure, then find that alcohol serves as an emotional suppressant in his early twenties, and eventually begin to drink to offset loneliness after a divorce in his thirties. The thirty-year-old man may look at the motives of his teenage self as silly and dismiss those who knew him then and raise the concern now.

**An example of B:** Addictions create problems, and problems become reasons to continue the addiction. When impaired, we neglect responsibilities. When responsibilities pile up, we get stressed. When stressed, we want the relief we believe our addiction provides. Or, when impaired, we hurt people. When we hurt people, there is conflict and guilt. Conflict and guilt become the reason why we need a break (often reengaging our addiction).

With these points in mind, you will be asked to think about each of your addictions in terms of multiple motives. As you examine the motives listed later in this chapter, place them in the chart below. Initially, use whatever terms are most natural for you to describe the motive. In Part Two of Step 3, we will offer a list of motives to consider.

- **Early motives.** These are the things that were initially appealing about your addiction. These are often the motives from when your addiction seemed innocent and fun. When you think about the "good old days" of your addiction, these are the motives that are usually at the forefront.
- **Later motives.** These are things you used your addiction for as it became more developed. These frequently represent when you felt like you were becoming "good" at your addiction and were mastering it. These are the motives that you use to convince yourself the addiction was useful.
- **Current motives.** These are the primary drivers for your addiction now. When you make the decision to break free from your addiction, these are the motives that tempt you to second guess this decision. When your commitment to recovery becomes weak, these are the things you say to yourself to convince yourself that recovery isn't worth it.
- **Self-perpetuating motives.** These are the problems your addiction "solves," but which it also caused. These motives usually still seem the most necessary because the problems are real, but your addictive-solution is the equivalent of throwing water on a grease fire.

| Addictive Substance | Early Motives | Later Motives | Current Motives | Self-Perpetuating Motives |
|---|---|---|---|---|
| | | | | |
| | | | | |
| | | | | |

- **Reflection:** What did you learn from placing your motives for addiction in this kind of historical sequence?

## G4 GROUP DISCUSSION: STEP 3, PART ONE

As you discuss this material in G4 group, these questions are meant to facilitate a more honest and beneficial dialogue about this material. Anyone is free to respond to whichever questions they choose.

### Experienced Members

- What skills of emotional regulation and conflict resolution have you had to learn or strengthen to make progress in recovery?
- What current motive was most difficult for you to release when you got serious about recovery?

### New Members

- How comfortable are you in admitting areas of weakness?
- What self-perpetuating motive is most intense for you right now?
- How can we pray for you?

### Everyone

- Has anyone relapsed this week? This first part of learning from a relapse is acknowledging it happened.
- What is a Romans 12:3 "sober judgment" of where you are in the process of recovery right now?
- Have you experienced a significant setback or victory since last meeting that you should tell the group?

# STEP 3

## PART TWO

### IDENTIFYING AND TALKING TO MY MOTIVES

The video for this part of Step 3 can be found at: bradhambrick.com/addiction3p2.

Our goal in the second part of Step 3 is twofold: (a) to put our motives into words more clearly, and (b) to find better words for responding to our motives. The benefit of putting our motives into words is that it allows other people to know us better and, thereby, support us more effectively. The benefit to finding better ways of talking to our motives is that it helps us end the white-knuckling style of change.

We will look at ten motives that are frequently associated with addiction. This list is not meant to be exhaustive but represents many of the alternative uses we try to derive from our addictive behaviors. If you don't find your motive on the list, then reading through the list should allow you to put into words what you're trying to get from your addiction.

1. **Social lubricant.** "Gateway drugs," like cigarettes, alcohol, and marijuana, tend to get introduced at a time when none of us feel socially competent or feel like we have access to the unwritten rules of relationships. Whether it is the disinhibition created by these substances or shared comradery of kids doing something bad together, addictive substances ease many of the insecurities that socially restrict us. Even into adulthood, many of us are uncomfortable being ourselves and think we need a social lubricant to have friends and be likable. A big part of overcoming addiction may involve being more comfortable being you and accepting your strengths, weaknesses, successes, failures, and quirks.

2. **Achievement.** This motive can be "Social Lubricant 2.0." Many of us battle through school trying to find our standout trait. We find we can't be the valedictorian, captain of the sports team, or prom king/queen. These take aptitudes we either didn't have or didn't cultivate. But it doesn't take much to be a world-class partier. Being a partier was a road to achievement that was attainable without sacrifice. We could be validated without any threat of anyone knocking us off our throne. Addiction seemed to be the easy road to greatness.

> A big part of overcoming addiction may involve being more comfortable being you and accepting your strengths, weaknesses, successes, failures, and quirks.

3. **Reward.** This motive requires some experimentation with AoD before it takes root. Once you begin to enjoy your substance of choice, it easily becomes your reward of choice. Have you worked hard all week? Have you finished a project or a test? Did you clean the garage or a closet? *As the addiction becomes stronger, the size of activity that merits a reward gets smaller. Soon everything is a reason to engage your substance of choice.*

   You do your addiction because you like it. —Ed Welch[1]

4. **Relaxation.** A step away from reward is relaxation. Now, we aren't looking to reward ourselves—we just want a break. AoD becomes a form of "me time." Addiction becomes our hobby. Instead of golf, shopping, fishing, crafts, or taking a nap, we engage our addiction. Our addiction is our way to unwind. *This is a scary transition because now, if we don't have our substance, it is no longer a good day because we can't relax.*
5. **Escape.** Beyond relaxation is escape. Now, more than our hobby, addiction is becoming our refuge. Addiction is where we run when life is hard. And, if we're honest, life is often hard—even without the complicating problems introduced by addiction. Life is full of drama. Life requires many skills that we're just not that good at (that's true for everyone, whether

someone struggles with addiction or not). There is so much uncertainty in life, so much waiting, and so much information we need but don't have. As we advance into addiction, every challenge becomes a trigger toward our substance of choice.

6. **Boredom.** With boredom, addiction no longer needs a reason. *When boredom becomes our motive, it is up to the world around us to give us a good reason not to engage our addiction.* At this point in the motive progression, the artificial high of addiction has rendered normal life to be boring. When normal becomes unacceptable or unbearable, addiction becomes the only option (at least that's how we experience it).
7. **Loneliness.** For some, perhaps many people, *addictions are more relational than behavioral.* Even if loneliness was not the initial motive, the isolation that develops as relationships deteriorate results in addiction becoming an attempt to fill the relational void. Addiction is like a friend-on-demand. The only problem is that addiction is a bad friend. When an addict is married, their spouse often is left feeling like the addiction is adultery. The addiction is trusted more than the marriage and the allegiance to the addiction is stronger than it is to their spouse. Even if you're not married, the same dynamic emerges with your close relationships.

   > It really is the case for the alcoholic that the good times are vacuous without alcohol, that the hard times are unbearable without alcohol, that loneliness doesn't feel lonely with alcohol, that loving relationships are mediated by alcohol, that success can only be celebrated with alcohol, that only alcohol can insulate from rejection and so on. To be an alcoholic is to enter into such a relationship with alcohol that everything else in life makes sense only if it is accompanied by alcohol. —Kent Dunnington[2]

8. **Cynicism.** When life seems arbitrary, addiction is the way many people quit in rebellion. When we feel like a game is rigged, our natural form of defiance is to quit. We demonstrate that we're not fooled by stopping. When we feel this way about life, then addiction becomes a form of opting out of the game.

When cynicism becomes our motive, we become highly resistant to people who try to convince us that it's worth it to engage recovery.

9. **Order.** This motive seems odd. We might think addiction creates disorder, but it would be more accurate to say that addiction creates dysfunctional order. Many of us struggle to meaningfully answer the question, "Why do I do the daily things I do? Why do I go to work, make money, keep house, etc., month after month, year after year?" In a culture where the only answer is "to do what makes you happy," the rituals and rewards of addiction can provide a satisfying (even if dysfunctional) answer to these kinds of questions.
10. **Punishment.** If we can't avoid pain, we weaponize it. A common use of pain is to punish. Some people use addiction to punish themselves, as a form of self-abasing penance. Other people use addiction to punish loved ones who disappointed them or won't do what they want. In this case, pain is not avoided by addiction, but harnessed.

    ▸ **Reflection:** What was missing? What motive(s) fit your addiction(s)? How would you describe what makes them enticing and what makes them ineffective?

▸ **Read Luke 9:23–24.** In light of what you've been learning about yourself, reflect on this well-known passage that summarizes what it means to be a follower of Christ. Often, we view this passage negatively, "You have to be willing to give up everything that's important to you in order to follow Jesus." But hopefully you can see the beauty of this passage now. What God offers through gospel-based self-denial is not punishment, but freedom. Through our addiction, we try to gain life but lose it. In Christ, God offers life if we are willing to deny ourselves and follow him.

▸ **Read Ecclesiastes** (yes, the whole book). The entire book of Ecclesiastes is one long book of motives for the pursuit of peace, hope, and happiness. As you read, realize this is the journal of a very wise and influential person. Realize your motives are not new, and neither is your disappointment with those motives. Be encouraged that someone has walked your same path, experienced the same emptiness, and learned where to find the security and fulfillment you're seeking.

## TALKING TO YOUR MOTIVES

We take the time to identify our motives to start healthier conversations—conversations with God, others, and ourselves. In the final part of Step 3, we will look at our internal conversations. In Step 4, we will look at our conversations with God, and in Step 5, our conversations with others.

> Addiction is like a friend-on-demand. The only problem is that addiction is a bad friend.

A large part of overcoming addiction is navigating conversations between your old self and new self (Ephesians 4:20–24), the spirit and the flesh (Galatians 5:16–24), or your sin nature and your new nature in Christ (Romans 5:12–21). The Bible speaks of this internal battle in many ways. Here is your basic strategy from this point forward:

- Recognize your distorted motives as belonging to your old self, which is bent on destruction.
- Express faith by doubting the messages of your old self.
- Challenge the messages of your old self with the truth of what God says about who you are.
- Make choices that honor God and contribute to your flourishing based upon God's truth.

Realize in this process that you have four options to address the messages from your old self or sinful flesh nature:

1. Agree and obey—a worst-case scenario
2. Disagree and obey—a step in the right direction
3. Agree and disobey—a further step in the right direction
4. Disagree and disobey—our desired destination of being healthy and free

These four options are represented in the chart below. What you see in this chart is that *you do not have to condemn yourself for hearing the destructive messages of your flesh. Instead, your goal is simply to disagree and disobey*. The part of you that clings to these destructive messages will slowly be put to death through faith and obedience. Don't allow a sense of condemnation over your flesh's continued presence to strengthen your flesh through guilt, shame, or a sense of failure.

**Figure 2. Talking to Your Motives**

| | Obey | Disobey |
|---|---|---|
| **Agree** | Most Dangerous: We believe what our flesh nature tells us about ourselves and obey what it tells us to do to make the situation "better." | Reality of Growth Step: There will still be times we are prone to agree with our flesh nature about ourselves, but even in these moments of weakness, we are able to resist the "remedies" our flesh offers. |
| **Disagree** | First Growth Step: We disagree with what our flesh nature tells us about ourselves but still obey what it tells us to do to make the situation "better." | Ultimate Goal: We consistently disagree and disobey our flesh because our confidence in what God says and what God offers is the strongest voice guiding our life. |

Pick one of the dominant motives for your addiction and fill in the chart below with what your internal dialogue is likely to sound like as you grow into the freedom God has for you.

| | Obey | Disobey |
|---|---|---|
| **Agree** | | |
| **Disagree** | | |

Use this chart to help you identify what your options are in moments of temptation. Take the time to articulate your four choices. Resist the urge to feel rushed by your temptation. Articulating your options not only makes the best choice clear, but it also puts you in the frame of mind to enact that choice. In times of temptation, call a friend in your support network and use this chart to allow them to get to know your inner struggle.

This four-quadrant exercise is included with the journal tool that is the focus of the next section.

## CAPTURING EACH STRUGGLE IN REAL TIME

*The overarching goal of Step 3 is to allow you to see yourself more accurately in real time.* When we experience temptation toward addiction, it is hard to see ourselves and our situation accurately. When our assessment is distorted, it is unlikely that our efforts at resolving these challenges will be effective. However, when we slow down enough to assess our situation, what seems impossible (i.e., sobriety) becomes possible with God's grace.

The journaling tool that concludes Step 3 is designed to help you do two things during each moment of temptation you experience:

1. Gather the relevant information you've learned to assess during the first three steps.
2. Gather information that will allow you to be better equipped to effectively implement the remaining steps.

A printable PDF of this tool can be found at bradhambrick.com/addiction.

This should be very encouraging. You can now begin attacking your addiction. Whereas before you likely felt like your addiction happened to you, now your addiction will not be able to manifest itself without you gathering important information that will become part of the remedy. The battle may still be hard, but the momentum is shifting in your favor. Press on!

## G4 GROUP DISCUSSION: STEP 3, PART TWO

As you discuss this material in G4 group, these questions are meant to facilitate a more honest and beneficial dialogue about this material. Anyone is free to respond to whichever questions they choose.

### Experienced Members

- As you've progressed in recovery, how have conversations with your old self motives changed?

- Which motive is stickiest and creates the most interference in your recovery?

### New Members

- Which motives stand out to as most influential in driving your addiction?
- How did the four-quadrant chart give you a more effective way to talk to these motives?
- How can we pray for you?

### Everyone

- What are the advantages to personifying your old self motives so that you talk to them more than embrace them as you?
- What was it like to read the book of Ecclesiastes in light of your addiction? What did you learn?
- Have you experienced a significant setback or victory since last meeting that you should tell the group?

## ADDICTION JOURNAL

Have you called your sponsor, accountability partner, pastor, or counselor? Yes No*

** Don't begin reflecting or writing until your answer to this question is yes. It is foolish to fight addiction alone.*

### STEP 1: ADMIT

**What was the situation?** Summarize the "who, what, before/after, and where" of your temptation toward addiction.

**How did I react?** Summarize the content of your thoughts and the choices you made.

Use the four-quadrant tool to identify both your actual reaction and other possible options.

What is my current commitment level to change?

Weak 1 2 3 4 5 6 7 8 9 10 Strong

### STEPS 2 & 5: ACKNOWLEDGE & CONFESS

**What are the most relevant components of "My Commitment to Change" plan?**

How willing am I to enact "My Commitment to Change" plan?

Low 1 2 3 4 5 6 7 8 9 10 High

**What are the consequences if I succumb?** For me? For others?

### STEP 3: UNDERSTAND

**What motives are present in this moment of temptation?** Circle or write in your motives/triggers.

| | | | |
|---|---|---|---|
| Social Lubricant | Achievement | Reward | Relaxation |
| Escape | Boredom | Loneliness | Cynicism |
| Order | Punishment | Other: | |

### STEP 4: REPENT

**How would God have me run to him in this experience?** What does repentance and faith look like *in this moment*?

### STEPS 6 & 7: RESTRUCTURE LIFE & IMPLEMENT

**How did I leave myself susceptible to this struggle?** What change is needed to prevent this from happening again?

**What actions would be most effective at thwarting my cravings and overcoming my addiction?**

**What aspects of this struggle do I need to share with a friend, pastor, or counselor?**

## Returning to God as Refuge from Substance as Escape

# STEP 4

## REPENT TO GOD for how my addiction replaced and misrepresented him.

At the end of this step, I want to be able to say . . .

**"My addiction is a counterfeit god offering an empty salvation. I am beginning to see why my addiction is offensive to God and the folly of trying to replace God with my addiction. I repent not merely because my addiction hurts other people and disrupts my life, but because God is superior to my addiction, offers a superior salvation, and lovingly enables me to love him (1 John 4:19)."**

# STEP 4

## PART ONE

### TO WHOM ARE YOU REPENTING?

The video for this part of Step 4 can be found at: bradhambrick.com/addiction4p1.

As you start Step 4, you probably feel like your soul has been laid bare. *Honesty is freeing, but it initially stings like the healing ointment placed on a wound.* You have been more honest about yourself, your behaviors, and your life than ever before. In Step 4, you are going to bring that honesty to God. You are not bringing God information that he needs in order to act. You are placing yourself in a position to receive what God has already done on your behalf.

*If you presume upon God's forgiveness* (i.e., "God has to forgive me. He's already sent Jesus to die. It would be a waste if he didn't follow through. Besides, God would be a liar if he promised to forgive and didn't honor his Word. I'll go through the ritual to get what's coming to me if that is what he wants."), *then you are not repenting.* You are making a legal transaction with someone you believe to be too stupid to know better. Additionally, you are leveraging God's grace in a manipulative fashion against others (i.e., "If God has forgiven me, why can't you?"). If this fits you, receive the strong warning of Galatians 6:7, "God is not mocked."

> There can be no secrecy between the soul and God, and therefore there can be no manipulation. —Gerald May[1]

*If you neglect seeking God's forgiveness* (i.e., "I don't deserve to be forgiven. I should have to pay for what I've done wrong. I've made enough people suffer because of my selfishness, so I shouldn't add Jesus to the list."), *then you are wallowing in self-pity and will remain in the same shame cycle that has likely fueled your addiction for a long time.* Relationally, you would remain an unsafe person who, by virtue of your self-pity, will manipulate others with your use of guilt.

The only way out of sin is through *genuine repentance.* All lasting change is built upon repentance. Repentance is when we change our primary allegiance from self to God. It is when we turn from trusting our ways to trusting God's ways. Repentance is when our primary goal changes from self-satisfaction and self-protection to glorifying God and loving others.

Who you pray to is more important than what you say.

Step 4 solidifies all the work you have done to this point and serves as the foundation for each step remaining on your journey. You have learned a great deal about yourself and your sin in the first three steps. It would be tempting to think this information would help you master and conquer your addiction. *Repentance is when we commit to quit trying to make our broken ways work and trying to do life in our own strength.*

The first question we will ask is, "To whom are you repenting?"

## TO WHOM ARE YOU REPENTING?

The identity of God is a significant point of controversy in Christian recovery circles. The generic "God of your understanding" that can be a chair or a doorknob rightly makes many Christians uncomfortable. This utilization of the "God of your understanding" phrase departs significantly from how Bill Wilson, founder of AA, originally used the phrase.

The original usage was meant to be an expression of humility, not universalism. Bill Wilson recognized that he, like all of us, had many misconceptions about God, and that as he pursued God these misconceptions would be progressively corrected. None of us has a completely accurate view of God when we first come to faith or begin recovery. We reach out to God as we understand him at that time. Like in any relationship, the depth and accuracy of our knowledge grows with time.

In this material, we do not believe all conceptions of deity are equal. We believe there is one true God, who stepped into time as the second member of the Trinity, Jesus Christ. He lived the life we were supposed to live, died the death our sin deserves, and is scandalously willing to offer us his righteousness for our surrender. Talking to any other god is a form of talking to ourselves and has the power of talking to a doorknob or a chair.

All of this is to say that what you believe about God matters. It doesn't just matter theologically, as if life was about passing a seminary quiz. It matters practically for your recovery. What you believe about God will determine whether you reach out to him for help and how you engage with him if you do.

In this section, we will look at common misconceptions about God that hinder our willingness to turn from our addiction toward God's care. Correcting these misunderstandings is more than an intellectual exercise. It is about cultivating trust more than learning facts. Placing an increasing amount of emotional weight on these truths takes time.

Knowing God is more than knowing propositions (i.e., God is all powerful, God is all knowing, etc.). Having a relationship with a president is different from knowing their name, hair color, and hometown. *As you build a more accurate understanding of who God is, you will find your prayers becoming more personal and conversational.* That doesn't mean you've been placing the wrong mailing address on your prayers, but that your knowledge of the person who lived at that address was skewed. God receives our prayers even when we don't know him well.

To whom you pray is more important than what you say. Too often we are not praying to the one true God who made us with a purpose and loves us beyond measure (Ephesians 2:8–10). Too often we think our words must convince a stingy God to be generous with us. Too often we believe that God is only paying attention to our lives when we mess up.

> What comes into our minds when we think about God is the most important thing about us. The history of mankind will probably show that no people has ever risen above its religion, and man's spiritual history will positively demonstrate that no religion has ever been greater than its idea of God. . . . We tend by a secret law of the soul to move toward our mental image of God. . . . The most [determining] fact about any man is not what he at a given time may say or do, but what he in his deep heart conceives God to be like. —A. W. Tozer[2]

What we want to do in this section is to debunk **four misconceptions about God** that make repentance seem either powerless or punitive. With each, we will provide counterarguments to help you see how a right relationship with God is foundational to enjoyable sobriety. When we don't know God accurately or rely on him fully, then other areas of life will necessarily begin to try to fill a role that is too large for them.

1. **God as unemotional.** *A primary reason we avoid repentance is because we think God is more concerned about what we've done (addictive behavior) than what we're going through (what we're escaping through addiction).* It feels as if God is only concerned about our sin and not our suffering. Our expectation of God's response to our repentance is him sarcastically saying, "What did you think was going to happen?"

    > The only master who is not harsh and enslaving is Christ himself. —Ed Welch[3]

    But think about the way your addiction is affecting you and those you love (Step 2, Part Three). Would God be loving if he was content for you to multiply these effects? God is concerned about your sin because it's multiplying your suffering. God couldn't love you and be content for you to remain enslaved to your addiction.

    God wants to bring comfort to the parts of your history that contribute to your addiction (history components of Steps 2 and 3). But you must trust him enough to forsake your self-destruction before you can experience his comfort.

► **Read Hebrews 2:14–18.** Notice how Jesus's compassion is central to the gospel. God was not merely concerned to pay the full price for our sin so that we could get into heaven (i.e., propitiation). God was also very concerned that we know he understands our struggles, so that we would want to be near him. Heaven is not meant to be an eternal all-inclusive vacation where there is so much to enjoy that we never get bored. Heaven is about being with our heart's desire, God himself, so the gospel must contain this kind of emotional-relational concern.

Do this thought experiment: Review the history of your addiction that you wrote out in Steps 2 and 3. Imagine reading this to God as a prayer. Now, in your mind's eye, look up. What expression is on God's face? Is he angry or compassionate; frustrated with you or concerned for you? Now read the end of Hebrews 2 again. Does your instinctual response accurately represent God?

2. **God as irrelevant.** Okay, so God cares; what can he do? God's not going to make the addictive cravings disappear. God's not going to instantly change my neurochemistry so that my brain doesn't feel like it needs my drug of choice to feel normal. So, I understand that God cares, but doesn't that still leave everything up to me and my choices?

   Yes and no. God won't change you against your will. God is a gentleman and will not force himself upon you. In that sense, everything is up to you and your choices. But *relationships enhance the number of choices that are available to us.* In isolation, you have the choices that your strength, wisdom, or abilities provide.

   When it's just you, it's your desire to be sober against your desire for your substance of choice. Good intentions are simply that . . . good intentions; what we know we should do until what we want to do trumps wisdom. When it's just you, it's your word against your word. Your voice, "I'm bored . . . hurting . . . worthless," competing with your voice, "Drinking will only make it worse."

   When God enters, healthy and happy no longer have to compete, because God's voice can serve as the final, loving arbitrator between our fickle desires. This doesn't mean we can't choose what is destructive, but it does mean we have more options than when we were alone and that we can pursue those options in God's strength.

► **Read Matthew 11:28–30.** In this passage, Jesus represents us as weary oxen carrying a load too great for us. He offers to share that yoke—the piece of wood fashioned to connect two oxen to a plow. God offers to come alongside us to offer his strength to our toils and to guide the process. It was customary practice in biblical times to pair an inexperienced ox with an experienced one, so that the older ox could guide the younger one to plow straight.

God's relevance does not eliminate our requirement to walk out the change process, but God offers needed strength and direction for the task that is too great for our strength.

3. **God as unpleasable.** If you view God as having standards that you are just unable to meet, you may give up. "I won't ever do it good enough for God. After all, doesn't God require perfection? There is no way I am going to be sober every day for the rest of my life. I get that God is beside me, but I know me. I'll stray even with a yoke connecting me to God. I'm an expert at wandering."

   It may be helpful to think of repentance as a commitment rather than a promise. God makes promises. He can keep them. We make commitments. Our repentance is not a promise never to fail again, but a perpetually renewed commitment to follow God and what he designed to be satisfying for our lives. When you talk about your struggle with addiction, speak of your commitment to this process rather than promise never to do "that" again.

   Realize that *God is pleased with progress as much as, often more than, perfection.* When God designed the Christian life, he decided to transform our character over time. This is something theologians call "progressive sanctification." This was God's idea and not a concession he made because we couldn't do any better. God, as the epitome of a good father, delights in the maturation of his children over time. He loves being part of the process of growth.

► **Read Hebrew 10:14.** Contrast the verb tenses. The ESV says God "has perfected" (past completed action) those who are "being sanctified" (ongoing action). This is not a contradiction, but a picture. Why is it that God is not so displeased with your failures that he would give up on you? He knows what he has already done in you. Why is God still calling you to faith and obedience? This is how he brings to fruition what he has already guaranteed. As you faithfully, yet imperfectly follow, God faithfully and perfectly keeps his promise.

4. **God as unapproachable.** Until you come to him, all these truths about God are merely nice thoughts. *We must approach God, or*

*we are alone with our addiction.* God is compassionate, relevant, and pleasable in Christ. This, however, does not remove your responsibility to come to him.

This is where many people pull up short. They learn many things about God. They learn how God feels about them and what he's done to make renewed relationship possible. But they don't come to him. For some this is failing to come to God for saving faith (initial salvation). For others it is a failure to come to God for sustaining faith (ongoing battle with indwelling sin). Either way, information is mistaken for relationship.

> It may be helpful to think of repentance as a commitment rather than a promise.

Think of a child with a favorite sports hero. The child could tell you that player's every statistic and piece of life history. But what they have is information, not relationship. If that player was the child's father, then they would play catch, shoot baskets, get ice cream, cry, ask questions, and just hang out. That would be relationship. Have you brought all of your life, not just your addictive struggle, to God in this way?

- **Read Hebrews 4:14–16.** Underline the phrase "with confidence draw near" (or the equivalent in your translation). Does this describe your relationship with God? God intends to be supremely approachable. If you did not have parents who were approachable in this way, it may feel odd to have this kind of father-child relationship with God. Don't allow that lack of familiarity to prevent you from embracing what God offers. Repentance is not punishment, it's not God putting you in time out to think about what you did. Rather, repentance is God's provision to allow restoration of the relationship he always intended to have with you.

- **Read Romans 2:4.** Notice that it is the kindness of God that brings us to repentance. This is what accounts for the sense of risk we feel. The outcome is guaranteed; God has already promised forgiveness. We hesitate not because we doubt the offer, but because we doubt the character of the one making the offer. Before moving to the next section on the key elements of repentance, realize that your ability to have this conversation will be directly proportional to how much you trust the character of the one with whom you're speaking.

▸ **Reflection:** How has this section challenged your view of God? How is God different from what you imagined him to be?

One of the main goals for this section has been to reduce the shame often associated with addiction. We often fail to deal with the guilt of addiction through repentance because we are paralyzed by shame. It may be beneficial to differentiate a couple of types of shame from the experiences of guilt and regret.

- Guilt is a sense of *legitimate condemnation* in response to sin. God resolves guilt through forgiveness, and we access God's remedy through repentance.
- Shame can be a *sense of identity* we take on as we allow our sin to define us. God resolves this type of shame by providing us with an identity greater than our sin, and we access God's remedy by continually embracing this new identity. Self-deprecating statements are a sign we're living out of our old shame-based identity.
- Shame can be a *sense of illegitimate condemnation* in response to suffering. God resolves this type of shame with comfort and acceptance, and we access God's remedy by entrusting God with our sorrows (Matthew 5:4). Addiction is often an alternative/empty remedy for this type of shame.
- Regret is a *form of grief* for a reasonable, good circumstance that was never realized. Addiction introduces many regret-based griefs into our lives. *God promises that the sweetness of future obedience is greater than the bitterness of past regret.* We realize God's promise is true when we grieve our regrets without allowing them to distract us from obedience.

As you get to know God for who he is, grow in your comfort of approaching God for resolution to guilt, shame, and regret. The best addiction can offer for these emotions is a temporary distraction that only makes the problem worse. Embrace the freedom from these painful emotions that God wants for you.

## G4 GROUP DISCUSSION: STEP 4, PART ONE

As you discuss this material in G4 group, these questions are meant to facilitate a more honest and beneficial dialogue about this material. Anyone is free to respond to whichever questions they choose.

### Experienced Members

- How has your relationship to honesty changed over the course of your recovery?
- How has your prayer life and view of God changed over the course of your recovery?

### New Members

- Which of the four common misconceptions about God creates the most interference for you?
- When you think about talking to God about your addiction, what expression is on his face?
- How can we pray for you?

### Everyone

- How have you seen the statement, "Relationships enhance the number of choices that are available to us," be true in your journey of recovery?
- Which devotional about the common misconceptions of God was most clarifying for you? What difference has this more accurate view of God made in your recovery?
- Have you experienced a significant setback or victory since last meeting that you should tell the group?

# STEP 4

## PART TWO

### WHAT IS REPENTANCE?

The video for this part of Step 4 can be found at: bradhambrick.com/addiction4p2.

There is no formula for repentance. It is not an incantation that only works if we say all the "hocus pocus, mumbo jumbo" words just right. Repentance is about restoring relationship. In that sense, repentance is much more like saying, "I love you," than ordering coffee from a barista. There are many ways to communicate your intent without messing up the order.

The six points below are meant to help you experience the full redemptive impact of repentance. In this sense, repentance and God's forgiveness can be like a smartphone. When we buy the phone, we get the features, but we do not get the full benefit of them until we realize they're there and how to access them.

After each point, we will offer self-assessment questions. These questions are meant to help you determine whether you are placing yourself in a position to receive the benefits God intends to provide through repentance.

1. **A desire to live for God and submit to his lordship.** Repentance does not begin with remorse. If that were the case, then we would be saying the cure for guilt begins with feeling worse. Repentance begins with a genuine desire to submit to God's lordship out of trust for God's character. *Repentance begins with the belief that what God wants for us is what is best. We trust God to lead our lives more than we trust ourselves.*

> If we don't surrender to Christ, we will surrender to chaos!—John Baker[1]

When we see God's ways as best, we are sorry we strayed from them. But this remorse is not "icky" like shame; instead, it is like the sense of reunion with a trusted friend after you realize you were wrongly upset with them and they graciously embraced the friendship again.

- ► Self-Assessment: Are you surrendering to the lordship of Christ because you trust his love for you, or are you only seeking relief from destructive habits?

2. **An understanding of how our sin sought to replace God.** *It is not just actions or distorted motives for which we repent. We repent for having replaced God.* Look back at Step 3, Part Two. Notice how the motives for addiction fill every role that God should fill in our lives.

> Repentance allows you to be honest and have hope at the same time.

The idols that fuel our addiction want to control all our lives—to interpret all the events and people in our lives. Repentance acknowledges this false worship as an affront to God and wants him to have his rightful place in our lives—allowing God to rightly interpret the events and people in our lives.

- ► Self-Assessment: Were you able to see the "God replacing" nature of your addiction? How did these idols distort the way you interpreted people and events in your life?

3. **A brokenness over the nature of our sin.** A healthy life begins with recognizing our fallen human condition. Ultimately, we sin because we are sinners. The myriad of factors that led to our sin are not the root cause. The root cause is that our nature has been distorted by the fall (1 Corinthians 15:21–22).

*True repentance is not just sorrow over our idols or behaviors but brokenness over our condition as a sinful person.* When we acknowledge our depravity, we gain an accurate self-assessment that motivates us to perpetually rely on God. Realizing that repentance is the perpetual need of every person allows for a non-shame-based honesty.

Repentance is what allows you to not be either fake or fatalistic about your shortcomings and ongoing struggles. Repentance allows you to be honest and have hope at the same time.

- ► Self-Assessment: Do you resist seeing yourself and allowing yourself to be known as someone who is in perpetual need of God's sustaining grace?

4. **An expression to God.** After sin, our pride or fear causes us to hide from God rather than talk to him (Genesis 3:8). Too often we think that a directionless sense of regret for sin is the same thing as repenting to God. That's not repentance; it's wallowing. It's not a conversation; it's shame-based reflection.

   You will not feel restored to God if you avoid him because of your sin. It does no good to address your repentance to "whom it may concern." Any ambiguously addressed repentance is little more than talking to yourself. Talk to God when you repent so that you can know his response to your repentance.

   - ► Self-Assessment: Have you talked to God in your repentance? If not, might it be that your repentance seems ineffective because the "no one" you spoke to can have no power to forgive or comfort?

5. **A belief in God's willingness to forgive.** Repentance is an expression of faith. We come to God with nothing to offer in exchange for our forgiveness. *If we do not believe God will freely forgive, we will continue in our approaches to try harder or hide more effectively, which allows our addiction to fester.*

   All this does is inadvertently reinforce the false beliefs that our sin is good and God is mean. Unless we believe that God is willing to forgive because of his grace and Christ's death, then repentance becomes a form of penance that is more like putting peace in layaway than receiving a gift.

   - ► Self-Assessment: How do you view God when you come to him in repentance? How has it begun to change since you began your work on Step 4?

6. **A new direction of life that begins with confession.** What this looks like will be clarified more in Steps 5 and 6. Think of repentance like marriage. Repentance is entering (or recommitting to) a covenant relationship with God. This is why sin is frequently called spiritual adultery (James 4:4).

   Repentance is our vow-renewal ceremony that expresses our renewed commitment to covenant fidelity. Marriage ceremonies and vow renewals are not done in private. They are public declarations of where our ultimate allegiance lies. This parallels why repentance doesn't remain private. It is also expressed through confession (Step 5).

   - ► Self-Assessment: Does it startle you to think of repentance as a vow-renewal ceremony? How does that image extend the implications of repentance beyond the moment of prayer?
   - ► **Reflection:** Do you think of repentance as an event or a process?

The answer is both. This is vital in using this material. When we think of repentance as only an event, we are prone to believe "We did it and it didn't work" when we continue to struggle with sin. How we come to faith—the event of giving our life to Christ—is also how we grow in faith—the lifestyle of repentance. We don't need Christ any less after our salvation than we did before our salvation. Whether you have been a Christian for decades or are still considering whether to give your life to Christ, this is important to understand.

As you reflect on the sample prayer in the next section, don't think of it as an outline of a speech (single event) that you need to perform before God one time to get him back on your team. Instead, think of it as a conversation (an ongoing process) that you will have with God daily as your relationship with him deepens.

## A SAMPLE PRAYER OF REPENTANCE

There is no magic in these words or this outline. The intent is to help you assimilate what you've learned to this point in your journey in a conversation of repentance with God before you begin having confessional conversations with other people (Step 5).

As you talk with God, review your notebook and verbalize what you have learned. Know that God is interested in what you say, not because you have finally learned your lesson but simply because he cares for you (1 Peter 5:7).

Heavenly Father,

I am glad I can come to you in the midst of my addiction. I have been hesitant to come to you, because . . .

*[describe your misconceptions about God and/or repentance]*

I also haven't wanted to admit the full extent of my addiction—to myself or to you.

*[describe what you saw about yourself in Steps 1 and 2]*

I am beginning to see that the things that have become more important than you (i.e., idols) are fueling addiction without providing the relief they promise.

*[list your motives from Step 3 and describe how you have lived for them]*

You know how those things came to be so precious to me. You know what I need (Matthew 6:8). Where my desires are good, I trust you to provide. Where my desires are bad or excessive, I ask that you change me in whatever ways are necessary.

*[talk about how this scares or confuses you]*

I have replaced you in my life with my fears and desires. I have declared myself more capable of caring for me than you. I see how wrong and foolish that is. Please forgive me.

*[talk with God about the six elements of forgiveness]*

Thank you for loving me and walking with me through these unsettling emotions (Psalm 23). I look forward to learning more about your character as I strive to trust and rely on you more in my daily life. Lord, grant me the perseverance to continue this journey even when I'm emotionally weary. Even though this road with you may be hard, the side roads without you are harder. I know this. Help me not to forget it. Amen.

## G4 GROUP DISCUSSION: STEP 4, PART TWO

As you discuss this material in G4 group, these questions are meant to facilitate a more honest and beneficial dialogue about this material. Anyone is free to respond to whichever questions they choose.

### Experienced Members

- How has your view of repentance changed in your process of recovery?
- How has repentance helped you escape the pattern of being fake or fatalistic about your addiction?

### New Members

- How is this depiction of repentance different from what you expected?
- Do you talk with God as honestly and conversationally as the sample prayer of repentance?
- How can we pray for you?

### Everyone

- Which of the six marks of repentance is currently most challenging for you?
- How has understanding that repentance is both an event and a process aided your recovery?
- Have you experienced a significant setback or victory since last meeting that you should tell the group?

The Courage of Honesty in the Pursuit of Sobriety

---

# STEP 5

## CONFESS TO THOSE AFFECTED for harm done and seek to make amends.

---

At the end of this step, I want to be able to say to others . . .

**"I have not represented God well in your presence.
[List ways your actions misrepresented God's character.]
You have been hurt by my ungodly
actions, attitudes, and beliefs.
[List ways this person has been hurt by you.]
My goal in life is to make God's character known.
That starts with this request for forgiveness. I value our
relationship more than my pride. I am currently working
on submitting my life to God's control, and I understand
if you need time to consider my request for forgiveness."**

# STEP 5

## PART ONE

### EXPANDING YOUR SUPPORT NETWORK

The video for this part of Step 5 can be found at: bradhambrick.com/addiction5p1.

*You will only be as free as you are honest.* Privacy kills change and fuels sin. Transparency kills sin and fuels change. Chances are this step may scare you as much as any step you have taken since Step 1. But remember, it is not nearly as scary to move forward as it is dangerous to go backward. Don't allow fear to make you forgetful.

When you are tempted to think, *This is not worth it. Too much is being asked of me. Why do I need to confess my addiction to others?*, remind yourself of these things. Our tendency has been to face difficult situations through addictive escape and avoidance. That can no longer be our life pattern. Now we will face hardship by being honest.

This honesty through confession serves two functions:

1. Acknowledging how we've harmed relationships, seeking forgiveness, and making amends.
2. Inviting people to become a more informed part of our support network.

Confession is what invites other people into our lives and points out where they can help. It is how we acknowledge our weakness and admit that we need their help; we won't lie, dismiss, or lash out. Confession is what ensures others that we have the humility and realistic expectations necessary to be safe to receive help. Put these things together and you realize, *confession is the door to community—the door through which we must pass if we do not want to be alone in the dark with our addiction*. That is what we will be doing in Step 5. We will begin the process of making our community outside G4 as authentic as our community inside G4.

## EXCUSES FOR NOT REACHING OUT FOR HELP

This section is a great gauge for your growth. *The less you embrace each of these statements, the more you have grown.* Remember the times in your life when you found each of these excuses convincing. Remember what your life was like then. Notice how your life has improved as you've relinquished these excuses. Use that as motivation to continue to distance yourself from these patterns of thought.

> Privacy kills change and fuels sin. Transparency kills sin and fuels change.

**Suggestion:** If these statements are still convincing, ask a friend to read these excuses to you. Hearing them spoken in the voice of someone you care about will help lessen their emotional appeal.

1. **"I should be able to handle this on my own."** *This is the Great Lie that undermines change.* We were never designed to live in isolation (Genesis 2:18). We were made for community. We would never accept this logic from a friend. But we are prone to believe it because it somehow makes us feel like we're being strong.

2. **"I don't want people to know."** At least now we're being honest in our excuses. The question is, "What do you want more: authentic friendship and freedom from addiction or a falsely positive reputation with your friends that you'll feel pressure to live up to?"

3. **"I am ashamed."** This one is even more honest. We feel less than when we acknowledge our struggles. But this excuse, like most fears, evaporates when we test it. When you confide in good friends, they admire your courage instead of condemning your weakness.

4. **"I don't want to be a burden."** Galatians 6:2 says Christians are to "bear one another's burdens and so fulfill the law of Christ." The more we listen to this excuse, the less the church is the gift of grace that God intends it to be. *When God gives you a weapon with which to fight your sin, it is not noble to lay it down before the battle.*

5. **"I don't have anyone to call."** Start by asking yourself, "How many people would be hurt to hear me say this?" If the answer is truly no one, call a pastor or Christian counselor as you begin to build quality friendships. If names come to mind, allow those individuals to be the hands, feet, and ears of Jesus that God intends his church to be.

6. **"People won't know what to say."** *You're not asking for answers; you're asking for forgiveness and support.* Another suggestion would be to ask them to go through this study with you. This would be a great way to review and reinforce the ground you've already covered within a deepening network of support.

7. **"By the time I realize I'm in trouble, it's too late."** The more you talk, the sooner you'll talk. Maybe the first few times you call, it will be after you've fallen. But if you establish the pattern of refusing to struggle alone, you will begin to call before the time when temptation has expressed itself as sin.

8. **"What if I reach out but still act out?"** You may. This is precisely why you're reaching out. This excuse is actually a great reason to follow the counsel of Step 5.

9. **"I tried this, and it didn't work."** Again, "work" can't mean "never struggle again." *Wise counsel only quits working when you stop trying.* Change is a process, and the process stops when you stop. When you are continually committed to making the next God-honoring, healthy choice in a context of good friends, it is working.

10. **"I'm not sure I want to stop."** If you're still uncertain about being willing to confide in more people how you're struggling, this is likely the root of the problem. Don't be ashamed of it. Be honest with yourself and weigh the consequences. Go back to Step 1 and assess yourself on the five stages of motivation, look at the consequences of not changing in Step 2, and ask yourself if your idols from Step 3 will ever keep their promises. Then realize these are not just conversations you need to have with yourself; they are conversations you need to have with some trusted friends.

- **Read James 5:16.** Notice that this command is given in the closing section of James's letter. It is a general call to every believer. *Unconfessed sin is abnormal in the biblical depiction of the Christian life.* When we experience as normal what Scripture depicts as abnormal, we should expect significant disruptions in our life, relationships, and emotions. Confession is one way we stop trying to make dysfunctional seem functional in our life.

## HOW TO EFFECTIVELY LET SOMEONE INTO YOUR STRUGGLE

Now we begin to turn the next corner. Once we are convinced confession is necessary, we need to determine who to speak with and how to prepare for these conversations. The eight points below will help you prepare.

1. **Begin with those you trust most and move out from there.** When something is hard, it is wise to begin where it is safest. Start with friends or family who you believe are most likely to forgive you for being deceptive and who are supportive of your continued journey. After these conversations, get feedback. Learn from each confession.
   - Who have you already told? Make a list. Recall how nervous you were in these confessions and the benefits these relationships have provided. Use this to assuage any resistance you may be feeling.
   - Who should be in your second tier of disclosures? Make a list.

2. **Don't dwell on their anticipated reactions.** The more time you spend imagining how the conversation will go, the worse it will get in your imagination. This is the natural human tendency for anything we want to avoid. Know what you need to say (Step 5; Part Two) and resist the urge to rehearse the conversation further than that.

3. **Be honest, simple, and concise.** Your opening statement should be as simple as, "*I have been addicted to [blank] for a while. I don't want to pretend like the struggle doesn't exist. I want to understand how it has harmed our relationship and ask forgiveness for the ways I've offended or hurt you.*"

4. **Disclose where you are at this point in your journey.** Confession is Step 5 of nine, so it's literally a mid-journey activity. Confession is not saying "I've arrived"; it's acknowledging you have a way to go. It would be appropriate to say, "I am at the point in my struggle where I am consistently resisting the urge to minimize my struggle but am still in the process of learning how to overcome it."

5. **Give your friend a quality resource on addiction.** Again, this study could be a resource you could point your friend to if they would like more information. It's available in an assortment of formats (e.g., written, video, and audio) for their convenience.

6. **Don't rely on just one person.** The smaller your support network, the more weight each person will bear. *You care well for your support network and increase the likelihood someone will be available in your moments of struggle when you allow your network to grow.* Meeting with a recovery group, pastor, mentor, or counselor who is experienced with addictions is also a way to improve the longevity of your support network.

Courage isn't the absence of fear; it is the continued pursuit of your goals in the face of fear.

7. **Be patient with yourself.** Making this list may feel overwhelming. That's okay. Change is never easy, and when we grow impatient with ourselves change becomes harder. Remain committed to taking the next healthy, God-honoring step, and you'll reach your destination.

8. **Be encouraged by your courage.** Courage isn't the absence of fear; it is the continued pursuit of your goals in the face of fear. You're doing that or you wouldn't have reached this point. That's not making lemonade out of lemons. It's affirming the sweat that came with your faithful obedience to God to reach this point.

► **Read Ecclesiastes 4:9–12.** This is often read as a marriage passage, but it is about friendship in general. Notice two things: First, this passage implies a mutual awareness of our struggles. Everybody in this passage is facing a challenge. Second, notice the number change from two to three. *When we obey God by reaching out to other believers in our struggle, God's presence is added to the impact of these relationships to magnify their impact.* When we entrust our struggle to a friend through confession, we gain more than the support of that friend. Ecclesiastes 4 teaches us that God is uniquely present in those conversations, strengthening the cords of encouragement and support being built with his presence.

## G4 GROUP DISCUSSION: STEP 5, PART ONE

As you discuss this material in G4 group, these questions are meant to facilitate a more honest and beneficial dialogue about this material. Anyone is free to respond to whichever questions they choose.

### Experienced Members

- What was the most significant, impactful, or difficult conversation of confession that you have had?
- How often does the Great Lie, "I should be able to handle this on my own," creep back into your thinking?

### New Members

- Which of the ten excuses is stickiest for you at this time?
- Who are your supports outside of G4?
- How can we pray for you?

### Everyone

- How do you respond to the statement, "You will only be as free as you are honest. Privacy kills change and fuels sin. Transparency kills sin and fuels change"?
- When have you recently mistaken courage in the face of fear as failure?
- Have you experienced a significant setback or victory since last meeting that you should tell the group?

# STEP 5

## PART TWO

### WHAT IS CONFESSION AND HOW DO I DO IT?

The video for this part of Step 5 can be found at: bradhambrick.com/addiction5p2.

Now we are making another pivot. Earlier in Step 5, we removed excuses and determined who we need to talk to. Now we will begin to identify what we need to say. We will do this by identifying seven common ways to undermine the redemptive power of confession.[1] With each example, we will define key action steps of confession that ensures confession has the redemptive impact God intends, both in your life and in the lives of those to whom you are confessing.

**1. No friend left behind.** One of the questions you have already examined (Step 2, Part Three) is, "Who has been affected by my addiction?" These are likely the people close enough to care about you, and you care about them. The general principle is, *if someone was impacted by your addiction, they should hear your confession.*

Remember, confession is not extreme, and it is not punishment. Those who really want to change involve others. Those who believe their change is good want others to know about that change. *Confession is an important transition from a temporary change mindset to a lasting lifestyle of change.* When we confess to those affected by our addiction, we are transitioning from managing the consequences of our addiction to transparent living in the pursuit of freedom from our addiction.

- ▸ Continue writing your list of the people you need to confess to because (a) they have been negatively impacted by your addictive lifestyle and (b) they will notice or be affected by the changes you need to make.

**2. No ifs, buts, or maybes.** These are words that radically change the nature of a confession. Grammatically, they are the "prepositions of blame-shifting and minimization." When you use them, the person you are talking to will likely be concerned that these words show you are regressing in your journey. But because you are trying to take an important step forward, you will be tempted to be defensive toward their concern.

Let's look at the impact of each word:

- *If* indicates that you doubt the certainty of what you're saying and, therefore, weakens your confession.
- *But* in the middle of a confession shifts responsibility from what precedes the "but" to what comes after the "but."
- *Maybe* reduces the level of personal commitment to what you are saying and gives little confidence to the listener.

Look at each of these examples and notice the impact of the three words in question:

a. "*If* I lied to you about my drug usage, I am sorry."
b. "I know I shouldn't seek comfort in alcohol, *but* that's just what people in my family have done."
c. "*Maybe* I could try to call you when I can tell I'm down and know temptation will be stronger."

This language is very common and represents the kind of tentative phrasing we fall into when we're uncomfortable. But it is also the kind of language that reveals a weak commitment to the change process.

► **Exercise:** As a way of learning to speak in a way that neither shifts blame nor minimizes your struggles, *rewrite each of these statements without the troublesome language.* Do the same with confession phrases you commonly use with words like *if*, *but*, and *maybe*. Write out the problematic version and then write a version without these prepositions.

**3. No generic confession.** One goal of confession is to help you be known accurately. When we know we're being fake, it is more tempting to buy into a false reality. When we minimize our struggle, if others respond accordingly, it seemingly confirms that our addiction isn't that bad. We interpret the calmness of those we've deceived as an indicator we're okay.

*Generic confession leaves us in control.* We have all the relevant information. Those we're confiding in aren't equipped with the necessary questions to ask. This leaves us vulnerable in the same ways we were before.

Being specific in our confession does two things: (a) it reveals to our friend that we are a safe person who can talk about needed changes in our life without falling into self-pity or blame-shifting, and (b) it helps us identify more realistic expectations of what change will look like.

> Confession expresses empathy and takes responsibility for the dominoes that result from our sin.

**Concentric circle exercise:** The exercise below is meant to help facilitate this aspect of confession and several other aspects of change coming later.

- In this exercise you want to identify the types of sin that emerge from each of the major motives that you identified as ruling desires in Step 3 (Ring A).
- From each desire, identify the specific actions or attitudes you are confessing. Write these in Ring B. We will explain the Rings D and E in the next point of this section.
- **Sample:** A sample web diagram is provided below using concentric circles. In this sample we will follow an addiction emerging from an exaggerated desire to escape.

A. Write each ruling **desire** you identified as too strong in your life in the center of a blank piece of paper.
B. Draw lines from that desire and write the sinful **actions** you committed to obtain this desire.
C. Draw lines from each of the actions and write the types of **occasions** when you have sinned in this way.
D. Draw lines from each occasion of sin and write the type of **impact** this had on friends or family members.
E. Draw lines from each impact and write the **evidence** of your sin's impact.

**Figure 3. Confessing the Patterns That Emerge from Addiction**

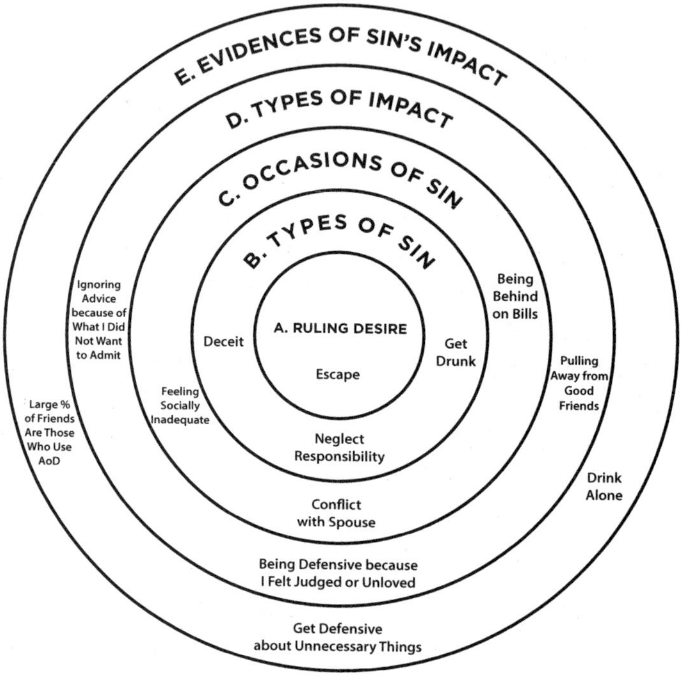


Notice how this exercise allows you to see the destructive life patterns that emerge from your addiction. Your confession should say more than, "I am an addict and I've hurt you." It should say, "I am beginning to see how my addiction explains many things in my life that I tried to blame on others or pretend were not happening. You are one of those people so, in addition to asking for your forgiveness and seeking to make amends, I would appreciate the opportunity to understand my life better by hearing your experience of me."

**4. No self-centered apologies.** Sin has consequences—both intentional and unintentional. Confession expresses empathy and takes responsibility for the dominoes that result from our sin. This is not groveling or penance, both of which are emotionally manipulative. Instead, it is owning the consequences we set in motion.

A key point to remember about the step of confession is that it's not about you. You take this step to care for those you've hurt and deceived. Self-centeredness and selfishness fueled your addiction. Confession is a vital part of living differently. By contrast, confession is an exercise in other-mindedness. *An unwillingness to express remorse for the consequences of our sin reveals that the self-centeredness that made our sin seem reasonable is returning.*

- Complete Rings D and E of your web diagrams if you have not already.
- Your goal in confession is to represent God more accurately to the person your sin has affected. God is compassionate and understanding to our hurts (Psalm 56:8). Therefore, our confession should include evidence that we have reflected on the impact of our sin on others.
- When sharing this aspect of your confession, avoid using verbs of completion (i.e., "I know . . ."); instead use process verbs (i.e., those ending in "-ing," for example "I am learning . . ."). Avoiding verbs of completion allows the other person to talk about other ways our sin has affected them without it feeling like they are piling on.

**5. No plea bargains.** Confession is not a plea bargain or the beginning of a negotiation. In your confession, the following things should be on the list of potential consequences with people in your life:

- "Because I see my need to change . . .
  - » I will no longer carry cash so that it will be more difficult for me to hide when I may fall."
  - » I will be transparent about my schedule so that there are fewer times when I feel alone and able to sin."
  - » I will forgo [activity, group, or friendship] because the temptation toward addiction is strong there."
  - » [Blank] allowed me to lie and cover my activities, so I will [discuss how you will remove that opportunity to deceive]."
- Write out other consequences that are more tailored to your struggle.

*Consequences are not punitive.* Consequences can play a disciplinary role (reinforcing life lessons and solidifying prevention measures) or a trust-building role (providing tangible fruit for an otherwise unverifiable desire to change). When we are confessing, our voluntary participation in the process means we should be viewing the consequences that are required as trust-building measures.

- Begin by stating the obvious. If there are clear changes you need to make, state them in your confession. Don't phrase them as, "I will do [blank] for you," as if it were a favor or concession, or "If you want me to, I will [blank]," portraying change as punishment. It is more in keeping with confession to say, "Because I see my need to change, I will [blank]."
- End by asking an open-ended question. *Honest questions are a sign of humility.* They reveal that we are not presenting a contract or deal, but that we are seeking to restore a relationship. A simple, "Are there other ways I can show you the sincerity of my desire to change or help you trust me?" would suffice.

**6. No words-only confessions.** Confession is not the culmination of the journey. It is merely drawing a map and acknowledging that the journey is needed. A lot of energy has been spent to get to this point, and that is why many people stop their travels at the step of confession. But when we stop at confession, our lack of future effort gives the person reason to say, "You didn't really mean what you said." This is why our study still has four more steps.

▸ **Read Luke 14:28–33.** *Part of embracing the gospel is counting the cost of following God and embracing the sacrifice.* Obviously, it's worth it. We give up our life of sin and its misery. In exchange, we gain a life of transformation into what God intended and an eternity in heaven. But it feels painful, and we often want to back out because of our doubt. The same is true with confession, because it is rooted in the gospel paradigm of dying to self and living for God's glory through serving others. As you prepare to confess, realize this dynamic is part of the emotional battle.

**7. No entitled or impatient confessions.** "I'm sorry" is not the same thing as asking for forgiveness. "I'm sorry" is an appropriate statement after a mistake. "Will you forgive me?" is the appropriate statement when we have sinned against another person. Be sure you are requesting forgiveness and not merely asking to be excused.

It is also important to remember that while forgiveness is commanded by God, Scripture never calls on the confessing person to remind others of this command. If your sin created mistrust in the other person, then you honor them by being patient. Impatience only exacerbates mistrust.

*While Scripture commands others to forgive, it does not appoint you as the timekeeper.* Allow at least as much time as it took you to come to repentance. It is hypocritical to expect someone else to process suffering (your sin against them) faster than you acknowledged and committed to change your sin. During the interval between confession and granting forgiveness, love and serve the other person while continuing to work on your personal change. This helps you remain other-minded and it honors your friend.

> Confession is not the culmination of the journey. It is merely drawing a map and acknowledging that the journey is needed.

## PREPARING FOR A CONFESSING CONVERSATION

Knowing what to say is different from communicating what you intended in the moment of conversation. In the previous section we outlined a conversation. In this section you will fill in the outline. *If we are used to hiding our addiction, then speaking with ownership and transparency may feel like speaking in a second language.* When we speak in a second language, we take more time to think through and plan what we intend to say.

At the end of this step is a tool to help you outline the conversations you need to have.

1. Begin with the list of people you created as you worked through the first point on confession, "No Friend Left Behind" (see page 101). Print one copy of the confession guide for each person on the list (PDF copies are available at bradhambrick.com/addiction).
2. The top paragraph is meant to overview the flow of this conversation. It does not need to be spoken but is a map to help you not get lost in the details.
3. Complete the open-ended statements that follow using your notes from earlier steps and your web diagrams.
4. If you are concerned about whether you succumb to blame-shifting or self-pity during your confession, rehearse confessing with a pastor, sponsor, mentor, or counselor.

5. Request a time to meet with each person and follow through with your confession.

- ► **Read Philemon.** This short letter tucked in the back of the New Testament is a prepared confession. Paul came to learn of how Onesimus, prior to becoming a Christian, had stolen from Philemon. Onesimus later became a Christian under Paul's teaching. Paul sent this letter with Onesimus when he returned to make things right with Philemon. So, if you are wondering if this kind of action is necessary or biblical, realize that it was important enough that God devoted a book of the Bible as an example of what you are preparing to do.

## G4 GROUP DISCUSSION: STEP 5, PART TWO

As you discuss this material in G4 group, these questions are meant to facilitate a more honest and beneficial dialogue about this material. Anyone is free to respond to whichever questions they choose.

#### Experienced Members

- What did you learn from your work in Step 5 that you wish you knew before you made your confessions?
- How did allowing time after asking for forgiveness impact those who were hurt most by your addiction?

#### New Members

- Which of the seven aspects of confession is most unsettling for you?
- What are the most immediate or obvious consequences of your addiction that you need to accept?
- How can we pray for you?

#### Everyone

- How has the completion of Step 5 felt like speaking in a second language? What are the most valuable things you learned from this exercise?
- How does reading the book of Philemon as an illustration of Step 5 impact your reading of this book?
- Have you experienced a significant setback or victory since last meeting that you should tell the group?

## CONFESSION GUIDE

**Name of the person to whom you are confessing:** ___________________________________

*"I have not represented God well in your presence [explain]. You have been hurt by my ungodly emotions, attitudes, and actions [describe]. My goal in life is to make God's character known. That starts with this request for forgiveness. I value our relationship more than my pride. I am currently working on submitting my life to God's control, and I understand if you need time to consider my request for forgiveness."*

**I am now willing to admit that I sinned against you by . . . [list specific sins and avoid words like *if*, *but*, and *maybe*]. These actions were my choice and were wrong.** Review Rings B and C of your Confessing the *Patterns That Emerge from Addiction* diagram on page 104.

**I am learning to see how much my life was ruled by the desire for [list motives for your sin]. You did not cause my sin.** Refer to the relevant motives from Step 3 and Ring A of your web diagrams.

**I am beginning to see how my sin has affected you. [Describe]** Describe what you can understand of how your sin negatively

**affected the life, emotions, trust, and relationships of this person. Refer to Rings D and E of your web diagrams.**

**I know I must change to honor God and to bless those I care about. Because I see my need for change, I will [list obvious needed changes]. I am still learning what other changes honoring God will require of me.** State those changes that are foundational.

**Are there other ways I can show you the sincerity of my desire to change or help you trust me in the areas where I've brought unhealthiness into our relationship? [pause and take notes on their answer]** This section should be blank until you speak with the person.

**I understand if it will take some time, but I am asking for your forgiveness. Thank you for showing me the honor of listening.**

# STEP 5

## PART THREE

### GUIDANCE FOR MAKING AMENDS

The video for this part of Step 5 can be found at: bradhambrick.com/addiction5p3.

In the Twelve Steps of AA, Step 8 asks you to make a list of all persons harmed by your addiction and be willing to make amends to each of them, and Step 9 asks you to make amends wherever possible *except when to do so would injure them or others*. These tasks are combined in Step 5 of this G4 curriculum.

The earlier sections of this step covered how to take ownership of your addiction, the need to see how your addiction affected others, and how to have a confessional conversation without blame-shifting, minimizing, or falling into self-pity. Now we will look at the final part of this step—seeking to restore what we can of what our addiction destroyed.

> In five words, here's the secret to making successful amends: *Do not expect anything back*! You are making amends, not for a reward, but for freedom. —John Baker[1]

Remember, making amends is meant to be restorative, not cathartic; you are not trying to get something off you (relief) but to make something more whole for others (repair). This is the reason for the exception in AA's Step 9. If you have doubt about whether your confession would be more harmful than helpful, then seek the guidance of a pastor, sponsor, or counselor.

As you think about making amends, it can sometimes be difficult to discern what to do for things that happened in the past or if the effects were less tangible. For that reason, we will consider **four types of amends**:

1. **Direct amends**. These are for tangible and measurable offenses. This is the clearest form of amends to make. *As you make direct amends, you are facing the history of your addiction in a new way. You are experiencing the impact your addiction had on others.* This experience should further remove any remaining tendency toward minimizing your addiction.
    - Example: Paying back money that you stole.
    - Example: Repairing property damage resulting from your addiction.

    ▶ Reflection: What are the *direct amends* you need to make and to whom?

2. **Narrative amends**. These are for offenses that result in damage in the form of mistrust or confusion. Now you are looking at the damage done via lies rather than finances or recklessness. To the degree that addiction is about escaping pain, *this form of amends requires us to grow in the maturity of facing the pain we caused.* This experience should further remove the self-centered form of thinking that often emerges during addiction.
    - Example: Owning and clarifying expressions of past slander both to the person slandered and the people to whom you slandered them.
    - Example: Clarify that damage to the relationship was because of your deceit or addiction—removing false guilt. Who are the people that likely feel responsible for things that were caused by your addiction?

    ▶ Reflection: What are the *narrative amends* you need to make and to whom?

3. **Living amends**. These are for offenses that can only be relieved by a commitment to healthy relating. Now you are looking at the damage done to hearts and relationships rather than bank accounts and property. If you have not realized it before, people love you and are affected by your self-destructive choices. *This experience should reinforce the importance of continuing this journey of recovery. You are giving people who love you hope. Your continued recovery protects that hope.*

- Example: Committing to authenticity with a friend or family member you closed out during your addiction.
- Example: Committing to a process of handling anger differently to someone you regularly lashed out at.

▸ Reflection: What are the *living amends* you need to make and to whom?

4. **Symbolic amends**. These are for offenses that are highly inaccessible but result in significant emotional disruption. Chances are these amends will be toward the parts of your addiction that haunt you most. *Admittedly, symbolic amends rarely provide as much closure as we would like. This experience helps us quit running from things we can't change.* By way of medical metaphor, these amends are for deep cuts. Embracing God's forgiveness makes them nonlethal. Making narrative amends removes the infection. But scars may remain. We can use those scars as tools to warn and teach others. We can allow those scars to remind us of the preciousness and frailty of life.
    - Example: If you killed a child in a drunk-driving accident, finding a way to serve parents in your church or community who have lost children.
    - Example: If your parents died before you began to pursue sobriety, perhaps you would write a letter to read to several of their close friends or to leave at their graveside.

> Making amends is meant to be restorative, not cathartic; you are not trying to get something off you (relief) but to make something more whole for others (repair).

▸ Reflection: What are the *symbolic amends* you need to make and to whom?

*This step can be one of the more emotionally painful steps to take.* Looking into the eyes of those you've hurt and hearing their experience (even hearing their forgiveness) can be very emotionally straining. That is why it is important to have a group, mentor, sponsor, pastor, or counselor guide you in this step.

Be patient with the process. When something is painful, our tendency is usually to either quit or speed through it. But both of these are addictive responses to an unpleasant event (even if substances are not involved). One of your goals in this step is to engage recovery with sober-mindedness (that is, with the mentality and life habits of someone not given to addiction).

As we conclude the instructional part of this step and you begin enacting it, it is good to remember the purpose of Step 5. We are prone to view this step as penance—a form of punishing ourselves for being bad, so we'll be less likely to be bad again in the future. This is *not* the purpose of confessing and making amends.

We confess and make amends to terminate the lifestyle of living as if nothing happened and imposing that lifestyle on those who love us. We acknowledge past sin and seek to mend its impact so that we, and those around us, can live cohesive lives instead of lives segmented by a collection of off-limits subjects and false assumptions.

This is the step when you realize that **John 8:32** is not an individualized truth. "You will know the truth and the truth will set you free" when you are not in control of the "truth" everyone has access to, but when you allow yourself and those around you to live freely without secrets, guilt, or shame.

- ▸ **Read Luke 19:1–10**. Notice that when Zacchaeus is convicted of a lifestyle of stealing and deceit, his first instinct is to make amends (v. 8). Don't get distracted by the numbers (i.e., half and fourfold). That would be using Zacchaeus's testimony as a prescription or recipe. Instead, notice that Jesus affirms this response in Zacchaeus (v. 9). It is not that making amends saved Zacchaeus, but the willingness to make amends was an expression of bearing fruit in keeping with repentance (Luke 3:8). As you complete Step 5, you are also bearing fruit that validates what God has been doing in your heart throughout this journey.

## G4 GROUP DISCUSSION: STEP 5, PART THREE

As you discuss this material in G4 group, these questions are meant to facilitate a more honest and beneficial dialogue about this material. Anyone is free to respond to whichever questions they choose.

### Experienced Members

- What was the most difficult amends that you needed to make?
- What was the most impactful amends you made and how did it impact you?

### New Members

- Are you prone to feel rushed and intimidated by this step? Be honest about that.
- Are you encouraged by the possibility of living a "less haunted" life?
- How can we pray for you?

### Everyone

- Are there amends you realized you needed to make that you have not made yet?
- In your own words, describe the difference between penance (what Step 5 is not) and refusing to live as if the past didn't happen (what Step 5 is).
- Have you experienced a significant setback or victory since last meeting that you should tell the group?

Establishing a Satisfying Sober Life

# STEP 6

## RESTRUCTURE MY LIFE to rely on God's grace and Word to transform my life.

At the end of this step, I want to be able to say . . .

**"To this point in my G4 journey, I have learned a great deal about myself [list with examples], my sin [examples], and my Savior [list with examples]. Because of these truths I want and need to make the following changes [list]. My temptation is to see these changes as a way to become independent from God and others, rather than cooperating with and celebrating God's grace in my life with others on the same kind of journey."**

# STEP 6

## PART ONE

### REMOVING TEMPTATION

The video for this part of Step 6 can be found at: bradhambrick.com/addiction6p1.

This is probably the step you were looking for when you started this journey. We intuitively want practical tips and strategies for change. These things are helpful and good. But they require a foundation to be effective. For five steps you have been laying that foundation of honesty and commitment, and garnering social support.

Now that you've laid this foundation, the strategies we'll discuss in Step 6 can be effective. You are no longer minimizing your struggle. You are being honest about your history. You have begun facing difficult emotions like shame, regret, and guilt instead of escaping them. You have people supporting you. With these things in place, the approaches we will discuss don't have to magically make your addiction go away. They can merely support and reinforce the honest life you're already living.

We will look at **five strategies** for restructuring your life to rely on God's grace and Word. Select the approaches that fit your struggle best. Don't feel compelled to try to incorporate everything we cover.

1. Removing temptation
2. Responding to unavoidable temptation
3. Strengthening your body and mind
4. Identifying healthy forms of fun
5. Strengthening your soul

As you prepare to work through this step, here are **three principles** to keep in mind:

1. *Change is not as complicated as dysfunction.* In Step 6, don't expect to read something profound. Lies are complicated; honesty is simple. In the same way, sobriety is a much simpler way to live than addiction. Because of this, we can be encouraged when these strategies don't have to be complex to be effective.
2. *You have more influence over your addictive experience than anyone or anything else.* We have emphasized the truth that we are powerless without Christ (John 15:5). We will now begin to emphasize the complementing (not contradicting) truth that God intends to deliver you in your day-to-day, seemingly inconsequential choices.
3. *Change plans must be (a)* ***acceptable****—something you voluntarily embrace, (b)* ***accessible****—feasible for your circumstances, and (c)* ***effective****—well-suited for your struggle.* As you select from the buffet of strategies below, allow these criteria to help you select the best-fit options for you.

## REMOVING TEMPTATION STRATEGIES

*The longer you have struggled with an addiction, the more things in your life become associated with the addiction.* Activities, locations, times of day, and people are just a few of the everyday things that get associated with addiction. One important way to manage your temptations is to rearrange your life to eliminate or limit your exposure to these temptations. Sometimes we must be strong by actively resisting temptation, but more often than not we should be strong by wisely avoiding temptation.

► **Read Matthew 6:7–13.** As you read this model prayer from Jesus, focus on verse 13. Your implementation of this section is a large part of God's answer to this part of the Lord's Prayer. One of the ways God "leads us not into temptation" is by providing wise principles in Scripture to organize our lives for avoiding predictable temptations. Pray for God to supernaturally limit the number of unpredictable temptations in your life. Obey God to radically eliminate the predictable ones (Matthew 5:27–30). We will look at **five areas of your life you need to examine**.

1. **Relationships.** Begin with the assumption that *no one in your life is neutral.* Ask yourself, "Does this person contribute to my recovery or my relapse?" List out the top ten people in your life who contribute to your sobriety and rank their influence on a 1–10 scale. Do the same for the top ten people who would contribute to your relapse.

   The overwhelming majority of addicts testify to the power of friendship as the single most important factor in their recoveries from addiction. —Kent Dunnington[1]

| Rank | Name | Influence | Rank | Name | Influence |
|---|---|---|---|---|---|
| 1 | | | 1 | | |
| 2 | | | 2 | | |
| 3 | | | 3 | | |
| 4 | | | 4 | | |
| 5 | | | 5 | | |
| 6 | | | 6 | | |
| 7 | | | 7 | | |
| 8 | | | 8 | | |
| 9 | | | 9 | | |
| 10 | | | 10 | | |

Evaluative Questions:

- Do you have at least ten people who are positive influences toward your sobriety?
- How can you invest in those relationships so that it increases the amount of positive influence they have?
- What have you been unwilling to relinquish that would decrease the number of negative influences in your life?

► **Read 1 Corinthians 15:33–34.** These are strong words that have direct implications for how much you interact with the people you listed in the right column. Many would object, "But wouldn't God want me to be a part of reaching these individuals? Isn't that the loving thing to do?" *The loving thing to do is to be an example of the freedom that Christ can provide and the choices necessary to pursue that freedom. You don't love them well by making their life seem okay or sabotaging your own recovery.* You love them by being a light on a hill (Matthew 5:14–16). If they want to take the same journey, invite them to be a part of your G4 group.

2. **Routes/routines.** Addictions make themselves at home in the rhythms of our lives. We use our substance of choice before or after parts of our day. We pick up our substance of choice on the way to places or events. For addiction to be life-dominating, these rhythms become very well entrenched. We no longer feel like we're doing them. They just seem to happen, like our morning routine before our coffee kicks in.

   Make a list of the routes and routines where your addiction can easily feel mindless. These are points when cravings are likely to feel particularly intense.

   - I have had the habit of using my substance of choice before . . .
   - I have had the habit of using my substance of choice after . . .
   - I have had the habit of picking up my substance of choice on the way to or from . . .
   - Other routines or routes strongly associated with addiction are . . .

   This is where your plan must be tailored to you. Examine your patterns and be ruthless in changing them (Matthew 5:29–30).

Changing these patterns begins with being honest about them instead of hiding them. Sometimes we hide a destructive pattern because we want to protect it just in case we need it. You don't need it. You need to be honest about it.

For patterns that cannot be eliminated, you need to make your support network aware. Raising awareness in your support network is an important way of feeling less alone in moments of temptation.

> Addictions make themselves at home in the rhythms of our lives.

3. **Household.** Where have you hidden or preserved access to your substance of choice in your home? Our homes should be places of rest and refuge. But, because addiction often degenerates into a private activity, our home becomes a place of temptation. *You restore your home to the refuge God wants it to be when you radically remove and disclose all access to AoD in your house.*

   This does not mean merely removing all alcohol from the refrigerator. But disclosing where you would hide your substance of choice to your spouse, parents, or roommates (whomever you share a residence with).

   ► Question: What changes or disclosures would be needed for your home to be as safe as possible from temptation? We are not trying to build a better mousetrap to resolve addiction. However, we are seeking to make every wise step possible to reduce temptation. Don't shortcut this part of the process.

4. **Irregular events.** Many one-time events are closely associated with your substance of choice usage: weddings, graduations, New Year's parties, birthdays, etc. Approaching these kinds of events is different from relationships and routines.

   ► Key Question: Are you willing to forgo attending any event that is unwise for your recovery? Yes No

This is the first and foremost question. If your answer is no, then irregular events are likely to derail your recovery. You will miss things that are important to you as you pursue sobriety. It is better to intentionally miss small portions of life than to miss large chunks of life because of addiction.

These questions can help you assess the wisdom of your attendance at irregular events where your substance of choice is likely to be.

a. **Awareness:** Have I talked about this event with people in my support network? If not, don't go. Have I minimized anything about the risk? If you are not being fully honest about it, then you shouldn't go.
b. **Journey:** Where am I in my journey of recovery? If my sobriety were an ankle injury and recovery a sport, would a doctor let me in this game?
c. **Support:** Will there be someone in my support network or someone committed to sobriety there?
d. **Energy:** Where are my current emotional and relational reserves? Am I walking into this event depleted?
e. **Plan:** Do I have a plan for how to avoid temptation and have accountability for key junctures at the event?

When considering an irregular event where your substance of choice is likely to be present, you need to discuss these questions with multiple people in your support network. If they think it's unwise for you to attend this event, you need to be willing to forgo attending.

These kinds of events are when we are prone to argue for folly over wisdom, which is a dangerous step toward relapse. However, because we haven't partaken of any of our substance of choice yet, we feel justified in downplaying the significance of this change in our mental and emotional attitude. If we won't heed the yellow flags, we tend to crash through the red ones.

5. **Simplify.** Less is more. *Stress is a near universal temptation to relapse.* We won't eliminate stress from our lives, but we can significantly reduce it by removing unnecessary activities and commitments from our lives.

   ► What activities or commitments in your life are contributing more stress than blessing?

Writing these things down doesn't mean they're bad. It just means they are likely a bad emotional investment during recovery. There are only so many things you can do well during each season of life. During this season of life, one of the big things you need to do well is recovery. This will require foregoing other things.

As you get to Steps 8 and 9, you will decide what things to reintroduce to your priorities as your recovery becomes more solid. Stepping away from excessive busyness will help you assess what things are most worth investing in when you get to that point in your journey.

> It is better to intentionally miss small portions of life than to miss large chunks of life because of addiction.

## G4 GROUP DISCUSSION: STEP 6, PART ONE

As you discuss this material in G4 group, these questions are meant to facilitate a more honest and beneficial dialogue about this material. Anyone is free to respond to whichever questions they choose.

### Experienced Members

- What was the hardest, but important, choice you had to make in removing temptation?
- What rhythm of your life is most different at this stage of your recovery?

### New Members

- Who do you have trouble acknowledging as one who contributes most to your addiction?
- What current rhythm/routine in your life is most important to change?
- How can we pray for you?

### Everyone

- Give an example of how "Change is not as complicated as dysfunction" is true in your life?
- From the Matthew 6 devotional, what choice do you need to make to remove temptation?
- Have you experienced a significant setback or victory since last meeting that you should tell the group?

# STEP 6

## PART TWO

### RESPONDING TO UNAVOIDABLE TEMPTATION

The video for this part of Step 6 can be found at: bradhambrick.com/addiction6p2.

Some temptation contexts cannot be avoided. However well we plan to avoid temptation—and we should strive to be excellent at avoiding it—we will need to be equally skilled at responding to temptations that we cannot avoid. That is the subject of this section.

One reason some temptations are unavoidable is that *temptation is a predator* (1 Peter 5:8). We don't have to look for sin; sin is looking for us. Even worse, *temptation is a chameleon*. Our destruction comes looking like a harmless situation. Like the pivotal scene in a scary movie, when temptation comes, the entire audience—anyone looking at our life—can tell its trouble, but we—as the main character—are prone to think we can handle it.

One way to deal with the folly of thinking we can handle temptation is **reframing**: temptation makes danger look enticing, but wisdom (rightly) reframes temptation as danger. We will consider five ways to properly reframe and respond to unavoidable temptation:

1. **High-risk moment plan.** You need a short, simple plan for moments of temptation. This plan should consist of fleeing temptation toward good people. Don't be cute or elaborate in your initial plan. Get away and get with people you can trust. This means you need to have several trusted friends on speed dial in your phone. This was the advice that Paul gave to Timothy about responding to any temptation.

> So, *flee* youthful passions and pursue righteousness, faith, love, and peace, *along with* those who call on the Lord from a pure heart. —2 Timothy 2:22, emphasis added

2. **Constructive self-talk.** *No one is more influential in your life than you because no one talks to you more than you do.*[1] What you say to you matters . . . A LOT! Often, temptation comes from within, from our own self-degrading thoughts. Even when temptation has an external source, what you say to yourself during a moment of temptation is pivotal to resisting it. During moments of temptation, our unproductive self-talk is usually either shameful or grandiose.

   An example of **shameful self-talk** would be:

   "I am such a loser. I can't believe I am weak and struggling again. I should have known better than to think I could be sober. Why do I believe such stupidly positive things? This is why I'm all alone. Everyone can see how pathetic I am, but me."

   An example of **grandiose self-talk** would be (usually before temptation):

   "I can handle this. If I don't learn how to handle situations like this on my own, then what good is being sober? I know what I need to do and am willing to do it. What is someone going to tell me that I don't already know? If God is with me, then why wouldn't I be able to handle that kind of situation? It's time to start living my life. I'm tired of being fearful."

> Temptation makes danger look enticing, but wisdom (rightly) reframes temptation as danger.

- Which of these two modes of self-talk are you prone toward?
  Shameful Grandiose
- What does your unhealthy self-talk sound like? Write out the common script.

A **constructive self-talk during temptation** would sound something like this:

"I know I need God every moment to live the life he calls me to live. I'm merely more aware of my need during moments of temptation. God promises that his strength is made perfect in my weakness. God is not annoyed by my prayers right now. He cares for me through my friends in moments like this. Thank you, God, for your presence, patience, and my friends" [then call a supportive friend].

A **constructive self-talk before temptation** would sound something like this:

"It is better to be safe than sorry. That means it is better to talk to a friend than assume I can handle this myself. False confidence is the most dangerous disposition I can have. I never see it until it destroys me. God protects me from false confidence through the people he's provided to walk with me. Freedom and confidence are not demonstrated by making cavalier choices, but through making wise choices. Whenever I feel that wisdom is limiting my freedom (I'm angry or resentful at wisdom's implications), I need to be most concerned and most honest."

► **Read 2 Corinthians 10:3–6.** Notice that the reframing exercises listed above are an example of "taking every thought captive." The moments in which you wrestle with destructive self-talk are the moments when this spiritual discipline is most essential. Use a T-chart, like the one below, to begin to counter key phrases or themes from your destructive self-talk. Take the destructive phrases you most frequently find convincing and put the biblical alternative into your words; that is, phrase it the way you would most naturally say it to yourself.

| DESTRUCTIVE SELF-TALK | CONSTRUCTIVE SELF-TALK |
|---|---|
| | |
| | |
| | |

3. **Relaxation training.** Temptation is stressful. Addiction is living in a state of perpetual, elevated stress. *Sometimes the unavoidable temptation we face is this increased stress we want to escape.* Unless we learn to manage stress well, we may defeat temptation in the short-term, but it will wear us down over the long haul. Our long-

term approach to addiction must include methods for managing stress.

> One's ability to cope with stress—in particular, with anger, frustration, boredom, anxiety, and depression—has been identified as a critical deficit area in many theories or models of addiction. —Carlo DiClemente[2]

Two forms of body relaxation are beneficial to alleviate stress. Each of these counters the negative physical changes that occur in our body when we are stressed.

a. *Breathing.* This technique may sound odd. But deep breathing can have a significant impact upon your experience of stress. One area that the body monitors to determine its sense of safety is the temperature of the nasal cavity. When the nasal cavity is hot, it triggers the stress response. When it cools, the body turns off the stress response.

   Think of the athlete who begins to breathe through his mouth as he runs. This causes his nasal cavity to heat up and triggers the adrenal system, which is part of the flight/fight stress response. Adrenaline provides an energy boost and intensifies his emotional state (hence the elevated reactivity of competitors at many sporting events).

   This is one reason many people feel relaxed when they smoke cigarettes even though nicotine is a stimulant. The calming power of rhythmically inhaling a cigarette is more powerful than the nicotine is energizing. Awkwardly, this means many smokers are as addicted to breathing as they are to nicotine, especially if their primary appeal to smoking is relaxation.

   When you feel stress mounting, it is recommended that you take a few deep breaths in through your nose (drawing in cool air) and out through your mouth (exhaling the warmer air away from your nose). This will cool the nasal cavity. It does not extract adrenaline already released but prevents the release of additional adrenaline. In this sense, it is the emotional equivalent of taking your foot off the gas pedal of your car more than stepping on the brakes.

b. *Progressive Muscle Relaxation.* Practice this exercise as we explain it. Flex the muscles in your hands, making a fist as you slowly count to ten (slows the pace of your thinking, which also offsets stress). Feel the slight burning sensation as lactic acid builds in your muscles. Release the grip after ten seconds. Now do the same with your forearms, then biceps, then triceps, then shoulders.

> The battle with addiction is largely a battle of attention; what you focus on will determine what you do.

As you do this, you are both focusing your attention away from your stress and countering the effects of stress in your body. The buildup of lactic acid in your muscles absorbs the chemicals that stress creates and causes our muscles to feel achy and tight after a time of prolonged stress.

As you do this with each muscle group from your hands to your feet, you are reclaiming your body from the effects of stress while willfully focusing your attention on what you choose.

4. **Distraction.** *Sometimes the unavoidable temptation we face is too much free time.* We have already calculated how much time our addiction consumed. If this time is not fruitfully filled, then it becomes part of the temptation back toward our addictive behavior. One way to fill this time is through distraction.

   Distraction is not used with a bad connotation here. During moments of temptation, the battle with addiction is largely a battle of attention; what you focus on will determine what you do. Focusing on the addiction, even resisting the addiction, during moments of temptation only feeds the intensity of temptation.

   After you've reached out to God and your support network for help (bringing temptation into the light), the best thing you can do is engage your mind with nonaddictive enjoyments—distractions. When you've done all that wisdom allows, temptation does not always immediately dissipate. After wisdom comes waiting. Passive waiting is dangerous.

   - Make a list of enjoyable activities or relationships you can engage in when vacant time is the impetus for your temptation.

These distractions should be readily available, enjoyable, and not contribute to temptation.

5. **Filling the void.** If distraction is for moments of temptation, filling the void is for the time between temptations. Overcoming addiction will create large segments of empty time in your life. How you manage these segments of time being vacated by addictive behaviors will go a long way toward determining your sobriety.

   If distractions are short-term activities, then filling the void is a long-term pursuit of hobbies. Filling the void is more about pursuing the life you want rather than occupying your mind during difficult times (i.e., healthy distractions).

   Fill the void, but don't overdo it. Don't allow addictive excess to distort how many or how much you engage new hobbies. *You want to engage healthy hobbies in healthy ways. You are leaving a lifestyle of excess.* Even the way that you engage new hobbies can be part of learning this new lifestyle.

   - ▸ What are one or two hobbies or interests you would like to pursue?
   - ▸ What would be indicators that you are engaging these hobbies or interests with excess?

   You may find that investing in mid-to-long-term goals, like cultivating a new hobby or skill, is as difficult as avoiding addiction. If that is the case, do not let it discourage you. It is another opportunity for growth. You are embracing a new lifestyle. You are learning the habits of sobriety. Give yourself the grace to learn and grow as you acclimate to this new lifestyle.

▸ **Read Matthew 12:43–45.** Don't be distracted by the mention of demons in this passage. Notice that when something destructive—a demon or addiction—is removed but not replaced, it creates a greater problem. Step 6, Part Two has been about filling in the void created by removing our addiction. The rest of Step 6 will continue this work. You have been digging addiction out of your life. That creates a hole. Now, you will begin the work of filling that hole with the God-honoring and personally satisfying things that will contribute to your flourishing.

## G4 GROUP DISCUSSION: STEP 6, PART TWO

As you discuss this material in G4 group, these questions are meant to facilitate a more honest and beneficial dialogue about this material. Anyone is free to respond to whichever questions they choose.

### Experienced Members

- What was an early indicator for you that you were learning a lifestyle of moderation?
- What have been the most effective ways you've learned to manage the physical effects of stress?

### New Members

- Is there a time coming up when you anticipate needing the 2 Timothy 2:22 escape plan?
- Are there any blocks of empty time coming up for you?
- How can we pray for you?

### Everyone

- What are the counter phrases for "taking every thought captive" that you've found most helpful?
- Complete this sentence: "The less I engage my addictive behavior, the more I will . . ."
- Have you experienced a significant setback or victory since last meeting that you should tell the group?

# STEP 6

## PART THREE

### STRENGTHENING YOUR BODY AND MIND

The video for this part of Step 6 can be found at: bradhambrick.com/addiction6p3.

In the previous section of Step 6, we considered how to respond to unavoidable temptations. This part of Step 6 is a derivative of that objective. Caring for our body well is another way to prepare for unavoidable temptation. Addictions tend to deteriorate our physical and mental health. This depleted health undermines our resolve to resist temptation and face hard things. That galvanizes the role of addiction in our life. Caring for our mind and body makes our life less hospitable for addiction.

- **Read Matthew 26:41.** Notice that Jesus ties the strength of temptation to the condition of the body, in this case fatigue. In the preceding hours, the disciples had traveled a long distance, secured a place to hold a ceremony, prepared an elaborate meal, eaten a meal high in carbohydrates, and then walked to a dark and quiet place to pray. When they repeatedly fell asleep, Jesus's response was, "Your spirit is indeed willing, but your flesh is weak." *There is comfort in knowing God is patient with our weakness, but we should also apply wisdom and avoid creating physical challenges that will heighten our temptation.* That is what this section is all about.

We will consider five forms of self-care that strengthen our body and mind. Your objective is to identify which one(s) would have the greatest impact on your physical and mental resilience. Consider these things a gift that God wants to give you rather than a duty that God expects you to fulfill.

1. **Consistent sleep.** Getting adequate sleep has a multifaceted impact on addiction. First, sleep restores our physical energy and self-control. These are vital to resisting temptation. Second, good sleep hygiene serves as an effective schedule regulator. An irregular schedule provides more opportunities for temptation to arise in moments for which we will be ill-prepared. Finally, being awake late at night results in boredom at a time when our support network is least available, and we are often most prone to succumb to temptation.

> Healthy eating choices are a form of self-care; addiction is a form of self-abuse.

   If possible, arrange your schedule to get seven to eight hours of sleep each evening between the hours of 10 p.m. and 6 a.m.

   If you are having trouble sleeping, consider the following suggestions to help with sleep:

   - Establish a bedtime routine to help habituate your body toward sleep. This routine should begin about an hour before you plan to go to bed and involve either doing or avoiding things that prepare your body to sleep.
   - Establish a deep, slow breathing pattern as you lay in bed that simulates sleep breathing.
   - Pray that God would give you restful sleep and believe he wants you to have it.
   - Memorize a passage of Scripture related to God's care for you and repeat it slowly as you lay down to sleep.
   - Play soft music or nature sounds that you can focus on to prevent your mind from beginning to plan or worry.
   - Reduce the level of caffeine and sugar in your diet, especially in the afternoon and evening.
   - Avoid daytime naps so that your sleep is in concentrated blocks; the physiological benefits of sleep are less when we break our sleep into smaller units.
   - Take a warm bath to relax your body.
   - Utilize progressive muscle relaxation and breathing exercises about an hour before going to bed.
   - Talk with a medical professional about the possibility of a sleep aid, disclosing your history with addiction and asking for non-habit-forming medical interventions.

2. **Balanced diet.** The addictive lifestyle is often a lifestyle of extremes. *The more areas of your life that you bring into intentional moderation, the less hospitable your life will be for addiction.* A balanced diet also has a multifaceted impact on the experience of addiction.

   First, healthy eating choices are a form of self-care; addiction is a form of self-abuse. Addiction doesn't care about your body. Making healthy food choices is a demonstration that you matter. Second, a balanced diet contributes to a healthy self-image and counters feelings of shame. Third, a balanced diet reveals that little choices matter. As you begin to experience the effects of these choices, your sense that your choices positively influence your life (self-efficacy) will grow. Self-efficacy is highly correlated with continued sobriety.

   In addition, *a healthy diet contributes to balanced emotions.* Where does our body get the component parts that comprise our brain chemistry? From our diet. If we recognize how much our diet influences our cholesterol, blood pressure, and energy levels, why don't we equally appreciate its role in our brain chemistry and emotional states?

   If you haven't already, implement the following practices:

   - Eat at least three meals each day at consistent times in the morning, around noon, and evening.
   - Have at least one serving of fresh fruit or vegetables at each meal.
   - Limit foods that are high in fat or sugar content. These can create blood sugar imbalances that enhance temptation.
   - Begin taking a multivitamin to offset any nutritional deficiencies that your addiction may have created.

3. **Physical exercise.** Like improving your diet, exercise also has the psychological benefit of being an emotional investment in your self-care. Exercise usually results in improvements in energy and appearance. It can also contribute to your sleep regulation. In this way, exercise contributes to all the other physical and emotional health benefits we've listed.

   Additionally, exercise triggers the release of the body's natural endorphins and dopamine, molecules people often seek to elevate to excess through their addiction. A consistent exercise program can be an excellent way to begin to reestablish your body's natural production of these pleasure molecules at healthy levels.

4. **Self-control exercises.** Addiction often results from, or at least produces, low impulse control. *Growing in impulse control is both an important part of overcoming addiction and a skill that is highly correlated with life satisfaction.* Impulse control is the ability to tell yourself no or wait and to obey.

   ▸ Make a list of the nonalcohol or nondrug substances and activities over which you struggle to exhibit impulse control. Perhaps it's certain foods, recreational activities, or social activities.

   Begin to intentionally practice moderation in one of these areas. Do not try to tackle them all at once. Predetermine what is a reasonable amount of time or quantity for the item you want to moderate. Tell a friend how you are seeking to grow and explain the impulse control goal behind this discipline. Begin to allow your recovery process to be about more (not less) than your substance of choice as you grow in self-control in a variety of areas in your life.

5. **Emotional endurance.** Working through recovery is a very emotion-laden process. As you continue to work through the latter steps of G4, you may begin to focus more intently on particular emotions that are prone to disrupt your recovery (i.e., anger, anxiety, depression, grief, etc.). Materials similar to this study are available for a variety of emotions at bradhambrick.com.

   Here is some general guidance to increase your emotional endurance:

   - *Continue to grow spiritually and intellectually.* Growth brings hope. It also brings fresh perspectives on these emotional challenges. *When you are intentionally growing, it is a sign that you have not surrendered to the hardship of life; that is endurance.*
   - *Always face the truth.* Retreating from the truth is a step back toward addiction. No matter how hard the truth may be, it is more liberating than a lie. Refuse to fall back into a life of

escape. Emotional escape (avoiding truth) is a precursor to substance escape.

- *Practice gratitude.* Grumbling is a very exhausting mental activity. Rehearsing your disappointments does not lighten or decrease them (Matthew 6:34). You may think that rehearsing your blessings is cheesy or a form of denial. But realize *there is an attractional quality to our attention; whatever we pay attention to we will notice more.* If you focus on your disappointments, you will notice more disappointments; the same is true for your blessings.
- *Forgive.* Sin must be paid for. But when you persist in unforgiveness, you are paying the penalty for the sins people have committed against you through the burden of bitterness you bear. The souring of your disposition becomes a temptation to relapse and is a drain on your emotional resilience.

Refuse to fall back into a life of escape; emotional escape (avoiding truth) is a precursor to substance escape.

> But holding on to that hurt and not being willing to forgive the person who hurt you in the past is allowing them to continue to hurt you today, in the present. —John Baker[1]

- *Live in the present.* God promises to give you what it takes to live each moment well (Matthew 6:25–34). Think of this like a "manna promise" (Exodus 16). God provided enough manna for each day. It was an act of faith for Israel to only gather what they needed for that day. Similarly, *living in the present is an act of faith in God's faithfulness to provide what you need each moment.* The obedience that emerges from this faith—staying in the moment—is a primary means by which God keeps this promise.

As you think about caring for your body as a way of strengthening your resolve and capacity to resist temptation, you should be encouraged. Don't get overwhelmed and start thinking about getting in the best shape of your life. Enjoy the reality that everything you do in this part of Step 6 is going to make you feel better. Receive it as a sign of God's love for you. *The things that God wants from you, in this case being a good steward of your body, he wants for your good.* Allow God's love for you to be a source of comfort and assurance on this difficult journey.

## G4 GROUP DISCUSSION: STEP 6, PART THREE

As you discuss this material in G4 group, these questions are meant to facilitate a more honest and beneficial dialogue about this material. Anyone is free to respond to whichever questions they choose.

### Experienced Members

- Describe the difference in your physical experience now versus when you were in your addiction.
- What aspect of caring for your body well had the biggest impact on your ability to resist relapse?

### New Members

- From the devotion on Matthew 26, how did you respond to Jesus's compassion toward our physical weakness?
- What form of caring for your body well would make the biggest impact on your ability to resist relapse?
- How can we pray for you?

### Everyone

- In what area of your life should you currently focus more on exercising self-control?
- Currently, how is your level of emotional endurance?
- Have you experienced a significant setback or victory since last meeting that you should tell the group?

# STEP 6

## PART FOUR

### IDENTIFYING FORMS OF HEALTHY FUN

The video for this part of Step 6 can be found at: bradhambrick.com/addiction6p4.

The goal of sobriety is not sobriety. If we fixate on sobriety, then our substance of choice is still at the center of our lives, except we focus on its absence instead of its presence. *We pursue sobriety to live a personally satisfying, God-glorifying life that is a blessing to those we love*. That means, at this stage in your journey (if not sooner), you should be intentionally setting aside time for things you enjoy.

This part of Step 6 is about identifying healthy, personally satisfying pursuits. As a result of your time in G4, we want you to enjoy your life more than you ever have before. We want the enjoyment to be more sustainable than what you knew during addiction and to be without the aftertaste of guilt, shame, and regret. That's why this part of Step 6 focuses on what you're running to—healthy delights—rather than what you're running from— addiction. This theme of running to something more than running from addiction will emerge more and more as you near Step 9.

To enjoy life, we must learn to savor the ordinary. This is the essence of contentment.

1. **Savor every moment.** Most of life is ordinary. Life will never be a series of epic moments. To enjoy life, we must learn to savor the ordinary. This is the essence of contentment, the secret Paul discovered to thrive in any circumstance (Philippians 4:11–12). Contentment is what gives you the freedom to enjoy every good thing in your life.

Get in the habit of periodically taking a deep breath, asking yourself the question "What is good?" and looking around for answers to this question. Follow that up with simple prayers of thanks for the things you notice. If you can do so without aggravating a tendency toward guilt, reflect on how many of these things you missed (i.e., didn't notice or didn't take encouragement from) during your addiction.

The opposite of addiction will not be highs that are the comparable equivalents of the highs of intoxication. Instead, the alternative to addiction will be the ability to enjoy the "mids" of day-to-day, normal life. While this may not be as exciting as many people would like, it provides a much more realistic goal.

- **Read 1 Thessalonians 5:16–19.** Consider this point an application of what it means to "give thanks in all circumstances" (v. 18), the spiritual discipline of savoring life. *Learn to savor God's goodness like you eat a good meal; not gorging it quickly without tasting it but enjoying each bite as a tribute to the chef.* Living out this discipline is a primary way we "do not quench the Spirit" (v. 19). In contrast to quenching, when we see and acknowledge the goodness God put in each moment, we are emboldening the Spirit in our lives.

2. **Engage your interests.** Ask yourself the question, "What did you enjoy before addiction began to dominate your life?" If you know the answer to that question, this section is for you. If you struggle to answer this question, then the next section will provide guidance.

   - Pause to Reflect: What things did you enjoy that were crowded out by addiction?

   How might you feel after reviewing the list you just made? You may feel robbed. If so, allow those emotions to further cement the notion that your addiction was never your friend. Everything you enjoyed about life was systematically dismantled to preserve your addiction.

   You should also feel free. Now that you are, by the grace of God, declaring your independence from addiction, you can pursue these interests again. A full and satisfying life is in front of you. You can't obtain it all at once. That is the false-high mentality of addiction. But you can begin to take daily steps in that direction while enjoying the entire journey.

► Reflect: What previous interest do you want to reengage? When and how will you begin to do this?

3. **Experiment with new interests.** Sometimes we have been in the bondage of addiction for so long that the things we enjoyed then don't fit our life now. Think of the mid-forties individual who began their addiction as a teenager. Teenage interests usually don't fit in midlife. Other times, we've changed enough that old interests don't fit. That's okay. We can still build a personally satisfying, God-glorifying life that is a blessing to those we love.

   How do we do that? Experimentation. Try a smorgasbord of healthy activities and see what you think. Be willing to try something you may not like just to find out if you like it. Think of life like eating at a new restaurant. You order something new to find out if you like it. Even if you don't, that's not failure. It's learning.

   ► Pause to Reflect: Whether your list under "Engage Your Interests" was full or sparse, make a list of things you *might* enjoy. Give yourself the freedom to brainstorm.

   One of the values for this list is that it can become cognitive filler for times of temptation. Boredom is a prime trigger for relapse (see Step 3). Anticipating or planning for a new, enjoyable activity can be a way to productively fill boredom. Even the anticipation of trying a new, healthy activity is part of the enjoyable life God has in store for you. Think about it: during your addiction you spent a great deal of time anticipating your next high (not just being intoxicated). *Anticipation is an important part of any pleasure. We want to learn the "discipline of anticipation" for our healthy pleasures.*

4. **Addiction jar.** Look back over your notes from Part 2 of Step 2. How much did you spend on your addiction per week or per month? This is money you invested in your addiction. Now we want to begin to make an intentional, financial investment in the new life we are creating.

Pick a percentage of the money you previously invested in addiction and put that in a jar. This does two things. First, it gives you a more tangible expression of how much you were investing in your addiction. Second, it provides funds you were already sacrificing that can be invested in serving those you've hurt or in pursuit of addiction alternatives.

*Warning One:* If cash is a trigger for you, modify this strategy by allowing someone else to hold the cash and let them know the goal you are using as an incentive to enhance your motivation for this journey.

*Warning Two*: You won't entertain yourself out of addiction. That is not the point. If entertainment is your primary goal, you are merely exchanging a self-destructive form of escape for a functional form of escape (that is still a worthwhile trade, but likely to lead to an addictive relationship with your new interests).

When we are rebuilding our lives after addiction, we often feel like we don't have the money to engage our interests. Taking a percentage of your previous investment in addiction and setting it aside to pursue healthy forms of fun is a way to maintain your motivation in recovery.

Allow yourself to dream for a moment. Much of your work in recovery has been hard. You've likely been weary many times. This part of Step 6 should feel like an oasis on your journey. In your personal Bible reading time, consider reading through the book of Exodus. Follow the ups and downs of God's people as they traveled from slavery in Egypt to the promised land. But also notice that God consistently held before them the goodness of the land he was taking them to—a land "flowing with milk and honey" as it was frequently called. Allow this part of Step 6 to be that encouraging enticement for you.

## G4 GROUP DISCUSSION: STEP 6, PART FOUR

As you discuss this material in G4 group, these questions are meant to facilitate a more honest and beneficial dialogue about this material. Anyone is free to respond to whichever questions they choose.

### Experienced Members

- Describe how your life has more joy now than it did during your addiction.
- What practices did you put in place to guard your use of money during your recovery process?

### New Members

- Is there anything discouraging for you about this discussion because it feels too far off?
- Does it seem realistic to you that life without addiction would be more enjoyable than life with addiction?
- How can we pray for you?

### Everyone

- Which interests would you like to rekindle that dissipated due to addiction?
- How has focusing on savoring life increased your level of contentment?
- Have you experienced a significant setback or victory since last meeting that you should tell the group?

# STEP 6

## PART FIVE

### STRENGTHENING YOUR SOUL

The video for this part of Step 6 can be found at: bradhambrick.com/addiction6p5.

In this part of Step 6, we are going to examine spiritual disciplines that can strengthen our progress in recovery. You will find that as you've gone through this study, you have already been incorporating most of them. However, at this stage in your journey, you want to make sure these are part of your life rhythms and not merely a side product of studying through these materials.

Also, we want to acknowledge we do not engage spiritual disciplines primarily for therapeutic reasons; we engage them to know and enjoy God. However, when engaged well, these disciplines have significant therapeutic benefits. That is the equivalent of saying, if you're married, you don't date your spouse to save money on counseling. But if you invest time and energy into your marriage, it does save time and money lost to unnecessary relational strain.

> We too are in danger of using Scripture as a practical "how to" manual, relying on useful principles rather than focusing on the crux of the gospel message. —Ed Welch[1]

Further, there are benefits that can be generally ascribed to particular disciplines. That is what we want to explore in this part of Step 6. We want to answer the question, "What unique benefits does each spiritual discipline bring to our journey in recovery?"

1. **Bible study.** *How much of the struggle with addiction is the bad content in our thinking (commonly referred to in recovery circles as "stinkin' thinkin'")?* This AA adage reveals the importance of the

content and tone of our thinking. Christians have long emphasized the importance of perpetually renewing our mind (Romans 12:2). This is not merely a recovery concept. It is a foundational part of sanctification (a.k.a., fancy word for spiritual maturity).

► Action Step: If you are not already in the habit of doing so, begin to set aside time each day to read and reflect on the Bible.

> We do not engage spiritual disciplines primarily for therapeutic reasons; we engage them to know and enjoy God.

For guidance on this spiritual discipline, consider the following chapters from these resources on cultivating spiritual disciplines in your life:

- Richard Foster, *Celebration of Discipline*, chapter 5
- Donald Whitney, *Spiritual Disciplines for the Christian Life*, chapters 2 and 3
- John Ortberg, *The Life You've Always Wanted*, chapter 10
- Brad Hambrick, "Four Ways to Read the Bible," (brief blog article available at bradhambrick.com/biblereading)

2. **Prayer and worship.** *How much of the struggle with addiction results from our thinking caving in on itself (i.e., shame, self-condemnation, circular reasoning, etc.)?* Our thinking needs an outlet and direction to be healthy. Prayer and worship provide direction for our thoughts. Prayer allows our inward thoughts to connect with someone who cares and understands. Worship provides a focal point for our thoughts (God) that is grander than our situation (addiction and its consequences) is bad. Prayer and worship are ways we can be positively awed by God's goodness and grace rather than negatively awed by the impact of our addiction.

> "Christian worship graciously displaces us from being the center of our story and instead incorporates us into the story of God." —Kent Dunnington[2]

► Action Step: Begin to have regular conversations with God. "Regular" means both normal words and on a consistent basis.

Don't get caught up in fancy words but just talk with God about your day as you live it.

For guidance on this spiritual discipline, consider the following chapters from these classic books on cultivating spiritual disciplines in your life:

- Richard Foster, *Celebration of Discipline*, chapters 3 and 11
- Donald Whitney, *Spiritual Disciplines for the Christian Life*, chapters 4 and 5
- John Ortberg, *The Life You've Always Wanted*, chapter 4
- Paul Miller, *A Praying Life*

3. **Silence, stillness, and meditation.** *How much of the struggle with addiction is our inability to rein in our thoughts or tolerate the discomfort of being alone?* Silence, stillness, and meditation are disciplines that tame the wild horse that is our thoughts and emotions. They are practices advocated by Christians for centuries because of their benefits for the life and character of believers.

> "Meditation forces us to reflect on the stories that we tell ourselves about our lives, and it therefore represents a very real threat to any addiction since it threatens to reveal the insufficiencies of those stories." —Kent Dunnington[3]

► Action Step: When you feel disrupted, pause. Take a deep breath. Be still and quiet your mind for thirty seconds. Allow this to be an act of faith that shows your trust that God cares about and is working in whatever is bothering you. Reengage whatever needs to be done next with the benefits of this stillness.

For guidance on this spiritual discipline, consider the following chapters from these books on cultivating spiritual disciplines in your life:

- Richard Foster, *Celebration of Discipline*, chapters 2 and 7
- Donald Whitney, *Spiritual Disciplines for the Christian Life*, chapter 10
- John Ortberg, *The Life You've Always Wanted*, chapter 5
- Esther Smith, *A Still and Quiet Mind*

4. **Journaling.** *How much of the struggle with addiction is the seemingly pointless disconnectedness of day-to-day life?* Life can easily begin to feel like a bad novel where one page has little to do with the page before it, and the story is going nowhere. Events keep happening, but they don't seem to be contributing to anything. This is what led Socrates to say, "The unexamined life is not worth living." Addiction responds, "Amen!"

   ► Reflect: How have your written responses to the prompts in this G4 study aided your recovery, been healthy for your emotions, and cultivated a greater sense of purpose in your life? If this facet of G4 has blessed you, be intentional about continuing it after you graduate.

   For guidance on this spiritual discipline, consider the following resources on cultivating spiritual disciplines in your life:

   - Donald Whitney, *Spiritual Disciplines for the Christian Life*, chapter 11
   - Brad Hambrick, Personal Journal for Spiritual Growth resource available at www.bradhambrick.com/journal

## CONCLUSION

Remember Step 6 is a buffet. The five parts of Step 6 have offered you twenty-three potential strategies to implement. No one could implement them all and maintain a healthy life. The intent is for you to select the strategies that best fit your life now and to have an arsenal of strategies to select from as your life changes.

For this step to be effective, you need to answer three questions:

1. **Which strategies** are more strategic for my continued progress in recovery? (Pick three)
2. **Why** is each strategy I selected important for my progress?
3. **What are the indicators** that this strategy is having its intended impact on my life?

If you have trouble identifying what you want to begin with, ask your fellow G4 members who are going through this study with you what seems like the best fit. This is a low-pressure choice. You can't really go wrong. Pick three. Implement them consistently for a couple of months. Then, you can evaluate them. The practice of being consistent and working toward a goal will be valuable, even if you decide a different strategy would be more advantageous later on.

## G4 GROUP DISCUSSION: STEP 6, PART FIVE

As you discuss this material in G4 group, these questions are meant to facilitate a more honest and beneficial dialogue about this material. Anyone is free to respond to whichever questions they choose.

### Experienced Members

- Which spiritual discipline has been most beneficial for your progress in recovery?
- How do you help prevent your spiritual disciplines from becoming lifeless and performed out of duty?

### New Members

- Did anything about this part of Step 6 come across as "just read your Bible and everything will be okay"?
- Which of the benefits described for each spiritual disciplines counter factors that contribute significantly to your struggle with addiction?
- How can we pray for you?

### Everyone

- How does the metaphor of dates and marriage counseling help you understand the importance of focusing your spiritual disciplines on cultivating a relationship with God more than focusing on the benefits?
- Of the overall twenty-three strategies listed (the whole of Step 6), what is your current top three and why?
- Have you experienced a significant setback or victory since last meeting that you should tell the group?

# STEP 7

## IMPLEMENT the new structure pervasively with humility and flexibility.

At the end of this step, I want to be able to say . . .

**"Implementing a plan is harder than creating a plan.**
**Trying to live out my plan has taught me more about myself, my addiction, and my Savior.**
**As I have had victory, the old expressions of addiction have taken new forms [describe].**
**Here are the unexpected challenges I faced [list],**
**how I failed [list],**
**where I succeeded [list],**
**what I learned [list], and**
**how God was faithful [list]."**

# STEP 7

## PART ONE

### RESPONDING TO RELAPSE

The video for this part of Step 7 can be found at: bradhambrick.com/addiction7p1.

As you arrive at Step 7, the momentum of change has probably already fluctuated several times. Getting started was hard. It felt like an uphill battle. Old patterns of life didn't want to let go of you, and you didn't want to admit they had a hold on you. Changing your addictive lifestyle can feel like betraying a friend; breakups are never easy even when they're good and needed.

But honesty with self, others, and God has a great way of building momentum. You began to let go of the weights of sin that clung to you so you could run free (Hebrews 12:1). This second phase is almost always exciting. When there are so many ways that your life can be healthier, it can bring a great sense of hope and progress.

In the third phase, the one we're starting now, life restructuring may begin to feel more like work again. *Implementation* is not an exciting word or process. *Lasting change happens in incremental units and mundane moments.* Change begins to impact moments that feel less relevant to your battle with addiction. The freedom you've gained tempts you to think you can risk a few of your previous bad habits.

In this step we will focus on three things:

1. Learning how to respond to relapse
2. Identifying markers of progress
3. Assessing life holistically to identify remaining areas of needed change

Note: It is recommended that you give at least two months to this step. You will need to see how your plan responds to the changes of settings, relationships, and emotions that happen over months rather than days or a couple of weeks. It is easy to move through Step 7 too quickly and not give it the attention it merits.

## DISCUSSING RELAPSE

*Is every slip a relapse? Does every bad choice mean I'm starting over? How can I not expect perfection for the rest of my life without making excuses that will make it easier to slip back into destructive behaviors?* You can see why relapse is such a difficult subject in a recovery program.

On one hand, you can expect to relapse many times in the journey of recovery. Learning from failure is part of the process. On the other hand, we don't want to expect to fail. We want to face every moment with the expectation that we'll rely on God to make healthy, God-honoring choices. We want to learn to live wisely in this tension rather than picking sides of the argument.

> Changing your addictive lifestyle can feel like betraying a friend; breakups are never easy even when they're good and needed.

With that said, here are seven expectations from G4 regarding relapse:

1. We will face relapse.
2. Relapse is the recurrence of self-destructive behaviors related to our desired change.
3. More dangerous than relapse is dishonesty and hiding.
4. Dishonesty and hiding are the difference between a relapse slip (short) and relapse slide (long).
5. Relapse begins to end when honesty begins.
6. We are more likely to be honest about something we've openly discussed.
7. We discuss relapse, not to excuse or predict it, but to place ourselves in a position for a healthy response.

To help prevent the first two expectations—(1) we will face relapse, and (2) recurrence of destructive behaviors—from derailing our progress, we will use a four-phase model for understanding relapse.[1] It is important to keep in mind that *experiencing an early phase in the cycle does not make the latter phases inevitable.* For this reason, we will look at each phase and ask two questions: (a) How do I realize I'm in this phase? and (b) What should I do at this phase to exit the relapse cycle?

1. **Phase one: change fatigue.** "I just want a break from working on recovery . . . having accountability . . . thinking about temptation . . . etc." This is the mild, passive-aggressive defiance of fatigue.

   It may mean that because of our progress in the present, we are downplaying how bad the addiction was in the past. This sets us up to make unwise, risky choices and resent those who caution us against those choices. It may mean that we're trying to do too much; we've added too much to our schedule too fast and, therefore, we want to cut corners on recovery to save time. This makes us feel like the people who caution us just aren't being practical.

   With this in mind, learn to pay attention to your unpleasant emotions: irritation, fatigue, stress, insecurity, loneliness, defensiveness, etc. These dispositions are often gateways to complacency. When you experience these dispositions, reach out to a member of your support network. *Being alone with these emotions can be as dangerous as being alone with your substance of choice.*

   *Honesty and listening are the two best responses to the complacency phase.* We need to be humbly *honest* about the internal resistance we feel. Don't give fake, nice answers to get people off your back. We need to *listen* to the concerns brought to us. It is likely other people will see the yellow flags we are prone to ignore.

2. **Phase two: convenient confusion.** Many people say, "Worldliness is what makes sin look normal and righteousness look strange." The further we get into temptation, the more this dynamic affects our thinking. You begin to view healthy choices as an unhealthy burden. You begin to view unhealthy choices as moments of freedom. You begin to view supportive friends as people who don't understand and expect too much.

   In the confusion phase we are usually still committed enough to recovery to say things like, "I know I should think/feel this, but . . ." The experience of confusion should make us humble, not confident; it should prompt us to move toward trusted people, not pull away from them. If your instincts are the opposite of this, consider it a major red flag.

*Honesty and increasing accountability to stay away from compromising situations are the best responses to confusion.* If you were dizzy, you wouldn't walk near a cliff. The same principle applies here. Call your G4 group leader, pastor, or a trusted friend and say something like, "I can tell my thinking is off. I may not want to hear what you have to say, but we need to talk."

> The experience of confusion should make us humble, not confident; it should prompt us to move toward trusted people, not pull away from them.

3. **Phase three: "acceptable" hedging.** We begin to think, *I deserve my self-destructive behavior*, falling back into the notion of viewing our addiction as a form of relief. The longer it has been since we used—meaning the longer it's been since we've felt the consequences of our addictive choices—the easier it can be to believe this thought pattern.

Frequent warning signs of the compromise phase are the following:

- Fantasizing about your addiction as "the good old days."
- Believing that you can use again without falling back into addiction (overconfidence).
- Displaying moody emotions and a selfish attitude.
- Reconnecting with your old friends from when you were actively addicted.
- Pulling away from or neglecting friends who have been part of your recovery.
- Being defensive when someone brings up changes in your mood, attitude, or actions.
- Neglecting your outlets for healthy fun or enjoying them less.
- Engaging healthy interests in excessive ways (i.e., excessive exercise, compulsive cleaning, etc.).

*Honesty and transparency are the best responses to compromise.* At this point, you are hiding things again. That should scare you.

Hiding never ends well. When we hide our choices, it transforms how we think. The people we're hiding our choices from are seen as being against us. But these are the people who love us most and want the best for us. That is why the courage to be honest by being transparent is essential to preventing compromise from becoming a catastrophe.

4. **Phase four: inevitable demise.** *Destructive choices destroy. There is no way around that.* When we fail to acknowledge how we start hedging (stage three), some life crisis will eventually get our attention. Don't allow shame or pride to prevent you from being honest about your choices.

   While our goal has been to interrupt the relapse cycle before it reaches the phase of life-altering consequences, the earlier in the deterioration process we acknowledge what is happening, the better. Until we are honest, things really can get worse. Don't believe the lie that they can't.

   *Honesty that is willing to accept consequences is the best response to a catastrophe.* We often fail to be honest about the catastrophe phase because we are trying to manage or mitigate the consequences of our choices. That is as futile as trying to put out a grease fire with water. It spreads the problem. What puts out the fire of a catastrophe is honesty; it removes the oxygen of deceit.

► **Read 1 Corinthians 10:13.** "God will not let you be tempted beyond your ability" doesn't just mean the type or intensity of temptation, but also means at any point in the temptation cycle. Too often we conceptualize a fictional point of no return in our battle with addiction. If a point of no return exists, it is the point at which we decide not to be honest with God, ourselves, and others. The grace of God means there is always hope in honesty. When God promises to provide "a way of escape" that refers to the opportunity for redemption and restoration to begin, not to the removal of all consequences. Restoration requires acknowledging the brokenness. That is as true for every relapse as it was at the beginning of your G4 journey.

## G4 GROUP DISCUSSION: STEP 7, PART ONE

As you discuss this material in G4 group, these questions are meant to facilitate a more honest and beneficial dialogue about this material. Anyone is free to respond to whichever questions they choose.

### Experienced Members

- What are some of your most frustrating experiences with relapse and what did you learn from them?
- What indicators of relapse in your life are most important for you to take seriously?

### New Members

- How many times have you tried to end your addiction? Has that discouraged you from trying again?
- How has your experience of addiction proven true the saying, "Worldliness is what makes sin look normal and righteousness look strange"?
- How can we pray for you?

### Everyone

- Which change fatigue emotions are you experiencing and would like to talk about?
- How did thinking about 1 Corinthians 10:13 in light of each phase of the relapse cycle change the way you applied this verse to your life?
- Have you experienced a significant setback or victory since last meeting that you should tell the group?

# STEP 7

## PART TWO

### MEASURING MULTIDIMENSIONAL PROGRESS

The video for this part of Step 7 can be found at: bradhambrick.com/addiction7p2.

Measuring progress is tricky for many reasons. Imagine it like trying to measure the ocean tide. Do you measure at the furthest point the water reaches? Do you measure the midpoint of each wave? Do you measure it by the point in the sand that is always underwater? Does the measure change if the tide is going out versus when it is coming in? Change with a life-dominating pattern like addiction has all these dimensions.

Prompt repentance is the key to stopping a relapse.

*Measuring progress with addiction is an attempt to measure something fluid and dynamic.* You can monitor behavior—was the drug of choice consumed? You can measure temptation—how strong are your cravings? You can focus on supplemental behaviors—have you been honest and transparent? Is sobriety from a substance with a defensive attitude toward supportive friends a good or bad thing? These questions help us see that we need a multidimensional approach to how we think about progress.

*Measuring progress tends to measure performance over dependence.* This tendency can easily begin to undermine the God reliance stressed throughout this G4 curriculum, as if we are going to master sobriety. Thinking we've arrived or that we've done so well that we don't need other people is a significant yellow (if not red) flag. Healthy recovery involves joyful dependence on God and healthy interdependence with other people.

*Measuring progress can foster shame when there is some type of regression.* How we handle regression is pivotal to establishing lasting change, hence the last section on relapse. We need a view of progress that gives credit for how we respond to our failures. Without this, our definition of progress fosters a culture of hiding and fakeness.

David Powlison gives **seven indicators of that progress** (bold text only).[1] Allow these to give you a more robust understanding of progress than merely counting the number of days since you last drank or used. As you read these, consider how each point helps you see and/or maintain progress even when you are tempted toward addiction.

1. **Decrease in frequency of sin.** Progress means we sin less. As you have worked through this G4 curriculum, there should be noticeable and quantifiable decreases in the frequency of your addictive behaviors. Whatever dimensions we add to our definition of progress, we are not detracting from or minimizing this one.

2. **Repenting more quickly.** Progress means we respond to temptation and relapse differently. Prompt repentance is the key to stopping a relapse. No longer will you give into the mindset, "If I've already been bad, I might as well enjoy it." We should now be convinced, "The quicker I am honest, the freer I will be."

3. **A change in battleground.** Progress means you see an advance in your battle against sin; from behaviors and belief to its core fortress—your heart commitments. These changes should excite you. This realization is what allowed Paul to say he was the "chief" of sinners without shame (1 Timothy 1:15 KJV). He was excited to take his battle with sin to its core. While each new battleground may require different strategies and durations of time to win, there should be a joy as you see God's kingdom penetrating new territory in your soul.

4. **Having a greater sense of need for Christ.** *Progress that does not persistently realize its reliance upon Christ degenerates into pride—especially for those who have struggled with addiction.* Pride is the gateway to a multitude of temptations. The point

is not to try to predict what form every new temptation will take, but to remain humble and joyfully aware of your need for Christ to live a satisfying life.

5. **Increased accountability and honesty.** Progress means that you do not need a reason to be honest and things do not have to be that bad for you to have accountability. In many ways, this variable is one of the primary, practical expressions of humility. Humble people refuse to fight sin alone and refuse to trust their own hearts apart from the community of caring Christian friends (Hebrews 3:12–14).

6. **Not responding to difficulty with addiction.** Difficulty is the time when progress is most clear. When we forget this, we become discouraged by difficulty and this discouragement adds to our temptation. Recognize that when difficulty comes (i.e., conflict, stress, setbacks, illness, etc.) this will be a time when your progress will be most evident. Realizing this should help you maintain the will to persevere during these challenges.

7. **Learning to love and consider the interests of real people.** This is the epitome of progress because it is the fulfillment of the whole law of God (Galatians 6:2). *The opposite of addiction is not merely sobriety. The opposite of addiction is the ability to care for real people and a willingness to be known by others in the ups and downs of real life without escaping.* We no longer categorize people as addicts like us or people too good to understand us. We don't disdain or fear people; we seek to love them. We don't misconstrue them to embolden our defense mechanisms; we seek to get to know them for who they really are.

    ▸ **Reflection:** Think of specific examples of when and how each of these indicators of change has been present in your life during the last three months. Give thanks for God's grace in each example. In each example, see the fulfillment of God's promise to be faithful and never abandon you in hard times (Deuteronomy 31:6; John 14:18).

These seven markers focus primarily on progress during the moment of temptation. They treat each temptation event as an independent event. This is a helpful perspective. It allows us to look at a **moment of struggle** and ask, "*How did I do?*" There is another perspective that is also helpful. That is when we look at **larger units of time** and ask, "*How am I doing?*" That is the focus of the sound wave image we will consider next.

A sound wave can be measured based on three dimensions: intensity, duration, and frequency. How loud was the sound? How long did the sound last? How often did the sound occur? To help you visualize this point, consider the illustration below:

1. Intensity (height: A to B)
2. Duration (width: Y to Z)
3. Frequency (peak to peak: 1 to 2)

**Figure 4. Addiction Temptation and Sound Wave Comparison**

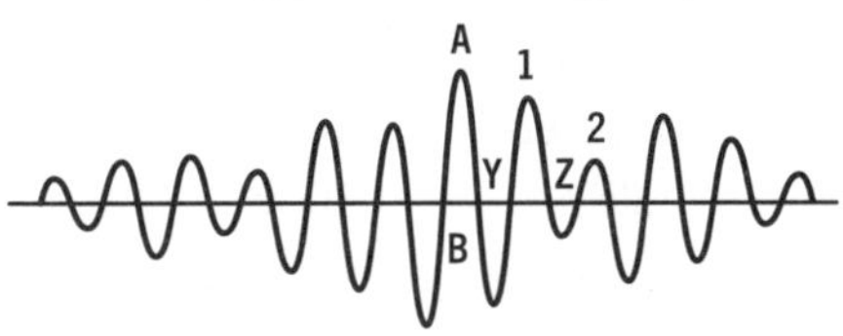


Our temptation toward addiction can be measured in comparable categories. This now gives you three more ways that you can begin to gauge your progress in recovery. Is your temptation *less intense*? Does your temptation last for *briefer periods of time*? Are your temptations *less frequent*? Your Step 3 journals should provide an objective basis for this assessment.

To provide some encouragement, consider the following "Life Disruption Score" (LDS). LDS is an arbitrary statistic, but it highlights a valid point. Let's assume that the intensity, duration, and frequency of your temptations were maxed out on a 1 to 10 scale. That would create an LDS score of 1,000.

10 (intensity) x 10 (duration) x 10 (frequency) = 1,000

Now let's assume that you decrease the impact of each variable by only two increments. How much do you think that would improve your LDS score?

8 (intensity) x 8 (duration) x 8 (frequency) = ________ (yes, do the math)

Are you surprised at what a small amount of progress in each area can do? It is not just a math trick. We tend to think about change by considering a terrible event and thinking, *If only I had done* everything *differently!* That equates progress with perfection. As we've noted, all-or-nothing thinking is addictive thinking. The sound wave metaphor allows us to see progress as temptation shrinks (as opposed to it vanishing).

> Difficulty is the time when progress is most clear.

Consider your last major episode of drinking, using, lying, hiding, and the subsequent fallout. What are the "moving from level 10 to level 8" choices you could have made in that situation? At how many points did your conscience temporarily prompt you to change, but you thought, *What's the point now?* How much differently would those events have transpired if you saw the value of making a level 10 to level 8 change? *If we see the value in making these changes, we are more likely to make them.*

From this part of Step 7, your goal is to see more dimensions of what progress is. The value in seeing the multiple dimensions of progress is to increase your motivation to make healthy, God-honoring choices in moments of temptation or in the early phases of relapse. *It is always possible to do the next healthy, God-honoring thing; and it is always worth it.*

- **Read Mark 8:22–25.** This miracle is unique because it happens in stages. The man starts blind (v. 22). Then his vision was partially restored (v. 24). Finally, his vision was fully restored (v. 25). In Jesus's ministry, miracles were often called signs because they were meant to point us to who God is and how God works. This miracle is a sign (i.e., picture) of how God works in our life. If we think, *If God is working in my life I'd be fully delivered. This step-by-step stuff means he's not working in me*, then we miss the point of this miracle. God often works incrementally in our lives. The work that

God began he promises to finish (Philippians 1:6). He promises to finish this work as we continue to remain invested in his agenda for our life (Philippians 2:12).

## G4 GROUP DISCUSSION: STEP 7, PART TWO

As you discuss this material in G4 group, these questions are meant to facilitate a more honest and beneficial dialogue about this material. Anyone is free to respond to whichever questions they choose.

### Experienced Members

- Can you remember a time when an all-or-nothing mindset toward progress disrupted your recovery?
- Which of Powlison's seven indicators of progress was most impactful in your recovery?

### New Members

- Before coming to G4, how would you have defined progress in recovery?
- What is your response to the following statement: "It is always possible to do the next healthy, God-honoring thing; and it is always worth it."
- How can we pray for you?

### Everyone

- How did the devotion on Mark 8 help you understand the value of this part of Step 7?
- What is your response to the following statement: "The opposite of addiction is not merely sobriety. The opposite of addiction is the ability to care for real people and a willingness to be known by others in the ups and downs of real life without escaping."
- Have you experienced a significant setback or victory since last meeting that you should tell the group?

# STEP 7

## PART THREE

### ASSESSING LIFE HOLISTICALLY

The video for this part of Step 7 can be found at: bradhambrick.com/addiction7p3.

Now that we have a more holistic picture of what progress looks like, we want to discern where we should expect to find it and continue to cultivate it. During the early phases of recovery, it is apparent what progress is and where to find it. In the later phase of recovery, these things can be less obvious, but are no less important. Incomplete work in the latter stages of recovery is like building a beautiful deck on your home and not sealing the wood. There is reason for short-term celebration, but the lasting benefits will be compromised.

Take a moment and visualize a mountain in your mind's eye. What do you see? Chances are that the picture in your mind is a snow-capped peak. This is the part of a mountain that captures our attention. But these peaks don't float. There are massive amounts of rock, dirt, and trees under those peaks. Similarly, when we think of addiction, we think of the worst moments. These peak moments capture our attention. But these moments don't float. There are many other unhealthy habits, values, missing skills, and insecurities under those moments. That is what we want to identify and root out in this part of Step 7. It is worth clarifying that in this mountain metaphor "peaks" are pinnacle destructive experiences that emerged from our addiction.

For this assessment, we will examine the who, when, where, and what of your addiction. Our goal is larger than just sobriety. We want to begin to make our life as inhospitable for addiction as possible by removing patterns of behavior that are not God-honoring or healthy.

## INSPECTION AREA ONE: *WHO?*

**Spouse:** *If you are married, then your spouse is either a significant asset or liability in your pursuit of sobriety.* Your spouse not only shares more space and time with you than anyone else, but they also navigate more challenges, stressors, and conflicts with you than anybody else. Your spouse will be more affected by changes in your lifestyle than anyone. If you haven't already, begin to share your journey with them.

- Have you been completely honest with your spouse about your addiction history? Are you currently living transparently with your spouse regarding your addiction?

If marriage enrichment is needed to create a home environment that is more God-honoring or home systems that are more functional and less stressful, you may find the *Creating a Gospel-Centered Marriage* enrichment seminars helpful in the areas of foundations, communication, finances, decision-making, and intimacy (available at bradhambrick.com/gcm).

> Marital problems usually get worse soon after the addict begins walking a path of change. —Ed Welch[1]

- If married, what are the aspects of enrichment that warrant attention in your marriage?

At this stage in your recovery journey, marriage enrichment and learning to manage life and conflict better will be an important part of your recovery process.

**Individual person(s).** Are there particular people who trigger heightened temptations toward addiction for you?

- Make a list of people who are a negative influence on your continued progress in recovery.

*If you have safety concerns* in this relationship, seek guidance from a supervisor, administrator, teacher, or other suitable authority figure over that relationship. If the relationship does not have a suitable overseer, then seek the guidance of a pastor or counselor. The book *The Emotionally Destructive Relationship* by Leslie Vernick can also be a helpful resource.

*If the struggle is rooted in insecurity rather than safety*, learn how to vocalize those concerns, learn social skills to overcome points of insecurity, and work on becoming less dependent upon this individual's approval. The resources below address various aspects of these concerns.

- *When People Are Big and God Is Small* by Ed Welch is good for relationships with a codependent dynamic.
- *The Peacemaker* by Ken Sande is good for those who are intimidated by conflict.
- *Navigating Destructive Relationships* is a resource in the G4 series for responding to relationships marked by abuse or addiction (bradhambrick.com/destructive).

**Group.** If your temptations toward addiction are attached to groups of people (i.e., those who have more status, better appearance, or some other marker you deem significant, etc.), then you need to examine the motivation and history for that reaction.

▸ List the groups of people who are emotionally disruptive for you.

Generally, temptations prompted by a group can be attributed to (a) an idolatrous overvaluing of certain desired attributes and social roles, (b) aspects of an abusive personal history that changed your instinctual response to those who remind you of the abusive experience, or (c) a prejudicial response toward that group of people.

▸ What is it about the groups of people that are disruptive for you that account for their emotional influence?

▸ **Read Galatians 3:28–29.** *Strong emotional reactions based upon group identification reveal that we are valuing things as most essential that are not most important about a person.* Our reaction reveals our preferences have become a strong measuring system. Part of the emotional, relational freedom the gospel provides is from the realization that we are all equally valued and equally in need of salvation by God. Our false systems of social hierarchy—believing that some people are better than others because of certain qualities we deem desirable—erodes the freedom this truth should provide.

**Role.** Sometimes our emotional reactions have less to do with a particular person than they do with the dynamic of the relationship or the responsibilities we bear in a particular position. If a particular role is preventing you from experiencing greater freedom from addiction, then it is important to discern whether it is because of (a) inadequate training or preparation to fulfill that role, or (b) the weight or significance that you place upon that role.

- What roles do you fill that create stress that increases temptation (i.e., parent, spouse, employee, confidant, etc.)?

*If a lack of training or preparation* for a particular role creates the angst that prompts temptation, then ask yourself the questions, "What training do I need?" and "How could I begin to pursue it?" Much of this study has prompted you to be proactive toward life struggles, rather than trying to emotionally manage them with substances. Continue being proactive by seeking the training you need to be more comfortable in the role generating stress.

*If you are overvaluing a particular role*, then you will have to wrestle with your priorities and values. Imbalanced priorities will crash even the best of systems. This means, however excellent your Step 6 plan for change may be, it will migrate back toward what you previously knew unless your values change. In this scenario, the type of insights that you gained in Step 3 on motives will be important focal points for your accountability relationships.

## INSPECTION AREA TWO: *WHEN?*

**Time of day/week/month.** Pay attention to whether temptation emerges at predictable times.

- Are there regular points in your day, week, or month when the struggle is stronger? If the answer is yes, then ask yourself, "What type of rhythm best accounts for this: sleep cycle, workload, social interaction, mealtimes, financial pay cycles, hormonal cycles, etc.?"

*If your addiction is linked to biological or time-related rhythms*, then it would be wise to consult with a physician (if you have not already) who could help identify how to regulate the body functions that account for these changes.

*If your temptations are linked to behavioral or social rhythms*, then, at the very least, you need to examine your life management systems. How well do you manage time and money? How willing are you to say no to overcommitment? If you find your mismanagement is rooted in bad priorities, which is often the case, then repent and commit to change. If the mismanagement is rooted in ignorance, commit to learn and commit to change.

**Season.** Seasonal or annual rhythms can be like day-week-month rhythms. Different seasons present different challenges. Summer has cookouts that are associated with cold beer. Thanksgiving, Christmas, and New Years have celebrations that often include substances that can contribute to relapse, break our life rhythms (which have become a source of protection), and create stress. It may be that in winter months you are more prone toward depression and tempted to self-medicate the unpleasant emotions.

► What seasonal or annual factors increase your temptation?

Seasonal temptations are predictable—talk with people in your support network about how you plan to face them.

**Energy level.** Fatigue impacts temptation to addiction. When we're tired, our capacity for self-control is diminished. Also, when we are tired, we often think we deserve a break or reward, which during times of temptation may still be interpreted to mean our substance of choice.

The questions below are meant to help you assess if your lifestyle is setting you up to have a consistent energy level, thereby reducing your level of temptations.

- Are you managing your life so that you have time and the mental freedom to get adequate sleep?
- Are you eating a healthy diet so that your body has what it needs to be nutritionally balanced?
- Are you getting cardiovascular exercise to help your body eliminate the chemical by-products of stress?
- Are you engaging in activities you enjoy so that your morale for a healthy life remains high?
- Are you using caffeine or other stimulants to offset unhealthy sleep habits?

- Can you thrive for the next decade if you live like you have for the last week? Month?

**Before/after.** The before/after might be an event (i.e., a work deadline, a visit to family, etc.) or interactions (i.e., conflict, time with in-laws, etc.) that are stressful or a letdown compared to your expectations. Learning to manage anticipation, disappointment, and achievement are important parts of maintaining sobriety.

- *Anticipation*—looking forward to a future event can create elevated stress levels for those who do not respond well to uncertainty.
- *Disappointment*—looking back at a past event that fell short of your expectations can increase temptation for those with a perfectionistic bent.
- *Achievement* may be a prompt for our addiction if we continue to think the reward should be our substance of choice.

▸ Look back over your recent temptation journals. Are there any significant before or after events that contribute to these temptations?

**Life transitions.** Major life transitions can also be times of emotional disorientation. Leaving for college, empty nest, first real job, becoming a parent or grandparent, midlife crisis, retirement, and similar transitions impact us in at least two ways: (1) they cause us to question our identity, and (2) they make it hard for us to know how we should feel or what we should do.

▸ What significant life transitions are coming up that you need to prepare for?

▸ **Read Ecclesiastes 3:1–8.** "For everything there is a season, and a time for every matter under heaven" (v. 1). God is not annoyed that we need to consider how these time factors impact our struggle with addiction. He knows we must pay attention to these kinds of factors because they contribute to our temptation. *God invites—even commands—us to make these kinds of assessments (Ephesians 5:16).* These evaluations are like a coach thinking through the strategy needed in each quarter or situation in a game, or a chef thinking about the food prep that already needs to be done at each stage of the cooking process. It is naive and disruptive to avoid this kind of evaluation.

## INSPECTION AREA THREE: *WHERE?*

**Home.** There are dynamics to homelife that are distinct from other locations. Home is where we get to relax and not be "on" anymore. Home is a place where we keep our stuff (meaning it is easier to hide and protect things at home). Home is often a place where we engage more comfort-seeking behaviors than anywhere else.

You can quickly begin to see how home will either be a great protection from or contributor to our patterns of addiction and why it is hard for home to be a neutral influence.

- ▸ What are the aspects of your homelife (routine and physical layout) that contribute to your addiction?
- ▸ What are the aspects of your homelife (routine and physical layout) that help alleviate your addiction?
- ▸ How or when can you refine or alter those aspects that contribute to your addiction?

If your homelife has a significant influence on your addiction, ask a friend or a counselor to review your answers to the questions above. Be sure that you are assessing what changes are possible and how to best accomplish them well. If addiction has been your normal experience, then it is likely that you may miss or over/underestimate the impact of potential changes.

**Work/school.** Outside of our homes, work or school is where we spend the most time and energy. Our occupation or education is usually how we answer the second standard question of social protocol—"What do you do?" *Our sense of accomplishment and identity, for better or worse, often emerges from these domains.*

- ▸ How satisfied are you with your current vocation and/or educational pursuits?

If you experience significant uncertainty and dissatisfaction with life based on your work or selection of schooling that would help you connect with a satisfying career, then the resources below may help you discern how to connect your vocation with God's general call to advance his kingdom in a way that is more purposeful and satisfying.

- *Every Good Endeavor: Connecting Your Work to God's Work* by Tim Keller
- *Step by Step* by James Petty (not about vocation, but an excellent book on the decision-making process)

**Activity:** Activities can become triggers for various temptations and insecurities. The weight that we place on our performance can become so significant that it becomes a reason to act out. How we perform in a sporting event, on an exam, at a task at work, or in front of particular people can easily become too central, forming our sense of identity and emotional equilibrium.

> Home will either be a great protection from or contributor to our patterns of addiction.

► What activities in your life are important enough to you to disrupt your emotions?

There is a simple axiom, "*Don't let what you do become the measure of who you are*," that is easier to understand than to live by. As we assess the role of activities on our temptation, we want to honor this axiom. In financial negotiations, people are advised to never lose their walk-away power. When they want something so badly that they cannot walk away, they will not get a good deal. Similarly, in emotional regulation never lose your walk-away power. When a moment becomes so large that you believe your future hangs on it, you will be emotionally crippled and compromised in how you respond to temptation.

► **Read Luke 9:23–25 and Matthew 6:33.** God does not want to withhold any good thing from you (Psalm 84:11), but God also does not want you to be owned by any good thing (1 Corinthians 10:23). When an activity becomes the source of your temptation toward addiction, then that is a strong indicator that this line has been crossed. Your joy will be greater in any activity when you are content in God without that activity.

## INSPECTION AREA FOUR: *WHAT?*

**Entertainment:** *One of the things we glean from our entertainment preferences is a gauge for what we consider ideal.* We entertain ourselves with things like romantic comedies, action movies, sports prowess, beauty, financial opportunities, etc. What we find engaging enough to captivate our attention reveals something significant about us. When these things move from entertainment to what gives meaning to our life, a problem emerges.

> God does not want to withhold any good thing from you (Psalm 84:11), but God also does not want you to be owned by any good thing (1 Corinthians 10:23).

- What does the entertainment you enjoy reveal about the things you value in life? Have these values grown to a point where they are marked by a sense of drivenness, fear, or inadequacy?

Some entertainment habits come with the expectation of our substance of choice. If you paired that form of entertainment with your substance of choice over a long period of time, it may be hard to think of that activity without it. In the early stages of recovery, we are usually willing to forego these forms of entertainment. At this stage, many people want to reintroduce things they enjoyed, thinking they can enjoy the entertainment without their substance of choice. For instance, they want to go to a stadium to watch a ball game and just decide not to have a beer. The risk of choices like this are difficult to assess.

- What forms of entertainment are strongly associated with your substance of choice?
- Are there some of these you want to reengage without your substance of choice?
- How can you mitigate the risk of relapse?
- Who have you vetted this possibility with?
- Did you become defensive or irritable during the vetting process?

**Albatross moments.** "Albatross moments" refer to occasions that deviate from your regular schedule; those occasions for which your instincts and habits may not be well-suited. *Albatross moments are often "more opportune times" that Satan uses to regain a foothold in our life (Luke 4:13).* We can't plan for albatross moments, or they wouldn't be albatross moments. But we can think through a response plan for times that catch us by surprise.

> Less frequent events and intense stressors are two critical types of triggers that must be negotiated successfully to sustain change and manage the Maintenance stage of recovery.
> — Carlo DiClemente[2]

- Remember: What are a couple of occasions when an unexpected moment resulted in reverting to addiction? Use these instances to help you identify the times you are preparing for.
- Reflect: What was it about the moments that you listed above that was most disruptive? Use this reflection to learn about yourself. *You can't scout the unknown situation, but you can know your response to uncertainty better.*
- Plan: What are the most important things for you to do when an unforeseen moment of temptation emerges?

## SUMMARIZING YOUR HOLISTIC ASSESSMENT

Review your notes from this part of Step 7. You have evaluated many areas of life. It would be easy to be overwhelmed by forty-seven little changes that you think would be good or wise. But that isn't sustainable and becomes impossible to track. Review your notes and look for common themes or overlaps in the kind of changes that would be wise. Become aware of the moments or setting when change is most needed. Focus your attention here.

## G4 GROUP DISCUSSION: STEP 7, PART THREE

As you discuss this material in G4 group, these questions are meant to facilitate a more honest and beneficial dialogue about this material. Anyone is free to respond to whichever questions they choose.

### Experienced Members

- At this stage of maintaining recovery, what areas of life are you focusing on most?
- How was working on the "lower two-thirds of the mountain" more valuable than you expected?

### New Members

- Later recovery is often a more detailed version of early recovery. What have you gleaned from this discussion that is valuable for where you are on your journey?
- What is different in how you heard fellow G4 group members talk about needed changes in their life than how you often feel about needed changes in your life?
- How can we pray for you?

### Everyone

- From the discussion on how we respond to different groups of people, how do you respond to people who have not experienced addiction? Painting them as naïve or better than us are two responses can limit our community to only those who have known addiction.
- From the devotion, what is your reaction to the statement, "God does not want to withhold any good thing from you (Psalm 84:11), but God also does not want you to be owned by any good thing (1 Corinthians 10:23)"?
- Have you experienced a significant setback or victory since last meeting that you should tell the group?

# Embracing Sobriety as "The Good Life"

# STEP 8

## PERSEVERE in the new life and identity to which God has called me.

At the end of this step, I want to be able to say . . .

**"I can see God's faithfulness over the last [duration of time in G4].**
**As I have experienced victory, my temptation has changed [describe changes],**
**and my ability to focus on God in non-crisis times has been stretched [examples of growth].**
**I have come to realize that *healthy* means more than the absence of addictive behaviors.**
**I am beginning to see more and more of the good things God wants for me [list].**
**Now that my life is about more than just not using, I am enjoying life so much more."**

# STEP 8

## PART ONE

### COMMON LIES AND DISTRACTIONS TO PERSEVERING

The video for this part of Step 8 can be found at: bradhambrick.com/addiction8p1.

As you begin Step 8, you should be enjoying life. Even if not quite yet, can you identify aspects of your life that are significantly better? Unless you can answer yes to this question and take delight in that answer, perseverance will be grueling. *Striving without delighting is exhausting.*

One of the keys to persevering, especially with a struggle as recurrent as an addiction, is the ability to enjoy an imperfect, in-process life. God does not just delight in you at the culmination of your sanctification. God delights in you right now. He invites you to agree with him that where he has you in this process is good. This provides the emotional stability and security to persevere in your journey of recovery.

With that as our starting point, let's ask the question, "What does it look like to continue to follow God from *here*?" The chances are that you've put so much energy into getting here that it may not be entirely clear how to prepare yourself for life after G4. What do you do when your life is not focused on overcoming addiction?

In this step we will look at *post-temptation temptations—those that uniquely arise when we're doing better.* In order to help you finish strong, we will look at three subjects for this stage in your journey.

1. How progress in recovery changes temptation
2. Preparing for transition from G4
3. Common lies and distractions

## COMMON LIES AND DISTRACTIONS

*Strangely, better is not always easier than worse. You likely knew the terrain of addiction better than you know the terrain of recovery.* That is the purpose of this section and the next—to prepare you for how challenges frequently mutate as you leave an old, familiar lifestyle for a new, unfamiliar one.

One of the most effective ways that temptation mutates is by introducing new lies (or revised versions of old lies) and distractions. As you read through this section, you should be preparing to listen to yourself. When you hear yourself thinking these kinds of thoughts, you should consider that a warning sign indicating that you should talk with your support network. The discussion after each lie is intended to give you truth and perspective to counter these unhealthy messages.

> One of the keys to persevering is the ability to enjoy an imperfect, in-process life.

**"I deserve a break. I have been good for a long time now."** When we talk about taking a break from our battle with addiction, it sounds very legitimate, but it leads to a return to addiction. *If you feel like you need a break, then it is important to make sure you are living a balanced, sustainable life.* "Break" language indicates we feel like we're sprinting rather than walking out a journey. We've tried to emphasize a sustainable-journey mindset from the beginning.

Often one of the contributive causes of addiction is unrealistic expectations about what you should be doing. Too often this same mindset is applied to recovery: an individual puts as much excessive effort into getting healthy as they did into their addiction. To persevere in recovery, we must engage recovery at a sustainable pace.

We can set ourselves up for relapse by picturing a perfect life we should be entering. When this happens, we feel justified in taking a break from what we perceive to be God's expectations and moving toward sin as our relief. *Unrealistic expectations are the kryptonite of perseverance.*

If, however, you assess your expectations and determine they are realistic but hard, then gaining the strength to endure and enjoy this lifestyle is what perseverance is all about (Romans 5:3–5; James 1:2–4).

Be sure to ask your support network to verify your assessment and ask for prayer or encouragement in this process of growth.

- How realistic are your expectations for your time, effort at recovery, quality of engagement with family, etc.?
- What adjustments need to be made—increasing or decreasing—in your expectations to make them healthier?

**"Now I can get back to focusing on what is important to me."** *What is important to me* can have two connotations. First, it can mean things that are legitimately important: things like family, work, or personal development. These are good. Second, it can mean things that used to be done in excess and contributed to your addictive lifestyle. These are bad. The cautions of this section are against this second connotation.

This distraction buys into the notion that overcoming addiction is merely about exchanging an unhealthy form of self-focus to more functional forms of self-focus. Sin never remains self-serving. But that is the way sin always likes to introduce itself, as your servant. But once it moves into your life, it mutates from servant to master. As you finish this study, several hours per week may be added to your schedule. We noted a similar time vacuum in Step 2. You want to take comparable steps to ensure you steward this time productively.

- Review your Step 7 work. What destructive aspects of excessive self-focus do you need to guard against?
- What God-honoring aspects of using your talents and loving people well do you want to engage more?

- **Read Romans 6:12–14**. In these verses, Paul emphasizes the idea that sin desires to reign over us. Sin wants to be our master, to have dominion over our lives. Before we became Christians, we were slaves to sin (Romans 6:20). Salvation removed sin as your master. We were purchased by the blood of Christ (1 Peter 1:19). Recovery has been about realizing the freedom that was ours in Christ. He had the rights to something we were not experiencing, like an unclaimed inheritance. Now, in Step 8, you are solidifying that freedom by refuting the lies that would lead you back into bondage.

Step 9 will also help you think through the God-honoring aspects of what is important to you. The life God designed you to live will be incredibly satisfying; it will fit you perfectly because it emerges from how God designed you. So do not be concerned that not focusing on what *was* important to you will result in a drab life. Allow the improvements in your quality of life from Step 1 to now be a confirmation of God's faithfulness from Step 9 and beyond.

**"This is not working, because temptation is still present. No one else has to work this hard."** Temptation only becomes easy (i.e., the sense of active resisting dissipates) when you stop fighting. But as soon as the weight of temptation is removed by succumbing, the greater weights of guilt and consequence are placed on you.

> No man knows how bad he is till he has tried very hard to be good. A silly idea is current that good people do not know what temptation means. This is an obvious lie. Only those who try to resist temptation know how strong it is. After all, you find out the strength of the German army by fighting against it, not by giving in. You find out the strength of a wind by trying to walk against it, not by lying down. . . . We never find out the strength of the evil impulse inside us until we try to fight it: and Christ, because He was the only man who never yielded to temptation, is also the only man who knows to the full what temptation means—the only complete realist. —C. S. Lewis[1]

Remind yourself that temptation is a sign of spiritual life. Only the dulling of one's conscience can remove the sense of temptation in a sin-saturated culture. In a culture of excess, we will perpetually be tempted to want more than a given moment, relationship, or salary can provide.

Resisting temptation can make us tired. But you can now view this fatigue as a sign of growth; like the person whose muscles are tired after lifting weights. That is a very different experience than the exhaustion of an addictive lifestyle. Before you were experiencing the consequences of an imbalanced life (i.e., expectations, activities, substances, etc.). What you are experiencing now is the fatigue of maintaining balance in a world that resists balance. The latter can be seen as a mark of God's grace rather than evidence of being at odds with God's design.

> Remind yourself that temptation is a sign of spiritual life. Only the dulling of one's conscience can remove the sense of temptation in a sin-saturated culture.

- What remaining moments or types of temptation are discouraging for you?
- How are these temptations an indicator of the growth and change in your life?

**"This is not worth it, because [insert desired outcome] is not happening."** It is easy to want to be healthy so that . . . But how we motivate ourselves is as important as what we accomplish with those motivations. Too often we want freedom from addiction for specific outcomes rather than for the inherent value of being free.

There may be outcomes from engaging recovery that you wished would be true by now that aren't. Maybe it's a key relationship restored or advancing in your job. It is okay to grieve that disappointment. But it is important not to allow grief to mutate into bitterness toward recovery.

Whatever you put in the blank—that is, "If I work through recovery, then I hope [blank] happens"—was never promised. If it is still absent, it is your addiction that created the damage that has caused the delay. It is not that God has failed you or been unfaithful to keep his promise.

You were promised freedom from the power and bondage of sin and addiction if you followed Christ. Your life is better for having taken the journey you have to this point. *In a world where we live in the tension of the already and not yet—what the gospel has already accomplished and what has not yet been realized—we often celebrate and grieve at the same time.* Allow God to comfort you in the grief over good dreams that have not been realized, and do not throw away the progress you've made.

- ► What are the good things you hoped for from recovery that have not yet happened?
- ► How are you protecting your heart from discouragement and bitterness? Who is helping you do this?

- ► **Read Ezra 3:10–13.** The context is the building of the new temple. Two sets of people were present: (a) those who had seen the old temple, and (b) those who had not. Group A was crying. Group B was shouting. God had done a good thing—restoring the temple. But the new temple wasn't as grand as the old one. There was a mixed emotional response. Notice that God does not condemn either. It was not wrong to grieve. But God did expect continued faithfulness. Falling back into the sin patterns that resulted in the old temple being destroyed was not okay. But grieving over disappointment was.

**"[Blank] situation is now more important than my need to be healthy."** Rarely would we say this out loud, or even allow ourselves to think it in these words. But this is the lie we believe when we place ourselves back in unwise or compromising situations for practical reasons. Practical becomes a user-friendly synonym for "more important."

- "I need to work more hours (get less sleep and spend less time with healthy friends) because I really need to get ahead."
- "I know this person is not emotionally healthy for me, but I miss them and think I'm strong enough to handle it."
- "I know events like weddings and New Year's parties were triggers for me, but I think I can enjoy it without slipping."

When you find yourself trying to alter or relax the changes you made in Steps 6 and 7, recall this lie as a red flag in your mind. This is why it was important for you to document the changes you made throughout this study. It needs to be clear to you when you are undoing the changes that provided freedom.

Those changes were *not* made to help you become strong enough to walk barefoot on enemy turf. Those changes were made because our enemy is stronger than any of us and can only be resisted on the home turf of God's wisdom. Do not fall prey to thinking that victory won under the protection of God's wisdom can persist when we fall back into the arena of worldly wisdom, often called common sense.

The best defense against lies and distractions is to understand the impact of living as if these lies were true. We don't want to be like a college freshman getting their first credit card and believing it's free money. The college freshman needs to understand that using a credit is spending tomorrow's money today. In Step 8, we've looked at lies and distractions that are equally important to our health and sobriety. Have the courage and maturity to call these lies what they are and avoid living as if they were true.

## G4 GROUP DISCUSSION: STEP 8, PART ONE

As you discuss this material in G4 group, these questions are meant to facilitate a more honest and beneficial dialogue about this material. Anyone is free to respond to whichever questions they choose.

### Experienced Members

- Which of these lies and distractions is strongest for you right now? What form does it take?
- What did you hope would be true at this point in your journey that isn't yet?

### New Members

- Can you see the importance of journaling as you study so you can look back on commitments you've made?
- Are you encouraged to hear the emphasis on cultivating an enjoyable life as a key part of recovery?
- How can we pray for you?

### Everyone

- How does C. S. Lewis's image of walking against the wind help you understand why the middle and later stages of recovery do not get as easy as we often think they should?
- Reflect together on your shared experience of the truth that "sin never remains self-serving."
- Have you experienced a significant setback or victory since last meeting that you should tell the group?

# STEP 8

## PART TWO

### HOW PROGRESS IN RECOVERY CHANGES TEMPTATION

The video for this part of Step 8 can be found at: bradhambrick.com/addiction8p2.

The premise of this part of Step 8 is that temptation changes as we make progress in recovery. There are a variety of reasons for this. But the key point is to avoid the assumption that past victory necessitates current victory. That is like the college student who assumes that because they made good grades in high school, excelling in college is a given. *New contexts require new skills and new awareness.*

Galatians 6:1–5 speaks to both the temptation of those who are "caught in any transgression" and the temptation of those "who are spiritual." Anyone who is in the latter category has spent time in the former; there are no saints who have not and do not struggle with sin. As you have moved from a new member of G4 to an experienced member of the group, you have begun making this transition. Below are **four new temptations** that emerge as we experience prolonged victory over addiction.

1. **Disappointment from new heights.** Poverty hurts differently when you've known wealth. *As you progress in recovery, recurrences of addictive behaviors create a stronger response of guilt and shame than you knew before.* We feel like we lost more, that we let more people down, or like we're starting over.

   When addiction was normal, it was less startling. It can be tempting to allow this intensified guilt to generate a major sense of failure and begin berating yourself. You must recognize (intellectually and emotionally) that God's grace is sufficient and necessary for falls from any "height" (in quotation because this is our category more than God's).

A protection from this temptation is to remember that spiritual maturity does not mean independence from God's grace (see next point), but a greater reliance upon it.

- ▸ **Read 1 Timothy 1:12–20.** Notice that toward the end of Paul's ministry he saw himself as more of a sinner than at the beginning (Acts 9). Paul uses this realization as an encouragement to young Timothy (vv. 18–20) because he realizes it is reliance upon grace that is the essence of his message—the gospel (v. 16).

- ▸ What are examples of you responding to disappointments and setbacks with greater despair?
- ▸ What are examples of you responding to disappointments and setbacks with greater maturity?

2. **Maturity and independence.** We are often deceived into thinking that spiritual maturity should cause us to be less reliant upon God. *So, God can focus on the people who are where we used to be*, we might think. This is a dangerous mutation in our temptation. It is like a great oak tree thinking its height means it no longer requires the soil. As soon as it detaches from the soil, its height only serves to quicken its fall and increase the damage that is done.

   Spiritual maturity can only be expressed as greater dependence upon God. Maturity requires this humility like trains require tracks.

   - ▸ **Read Galatians 2:18–21.** Notice that Paul warns against rebuilding what was torn down (v. 18). *This is exactly what a false view of maturity does.* It is from this warning that Paul lays down the principle that maturity is less of me and more of Christ (v. 20). Like a caterpillar matures into a butterfly, we are called to mature into something different from what we started. We started grounded and crawling in our independence from God (the essence of sin). We mature into people who realize dependence upon God is freedom, like the butterfly finds freedom allowing its wings to ride a summer breeze. The caterpillar must die to become a butterfly. The butterfly must trust the breeze to fly. As we overcome addiction, we allow the old man to die to become who God made us to be and rely on his grace to propel us into the next seasons of life.

- How are you beginning to see maturity as being synonymous with greater dependence on God?

3. **Pressure of new opportunities.** With growth comes opportunity, and not necessarily because we are seeking it. Managing your life well almost inevitably brings more opportunities to speak into the lives of others. We may be excited or intimidated by the opportunities that begin to come our way. But we can be sure that with maturity will come opportunities to offer others the same hope we have received (2 Corinthians 1:3–5).

   - Keep a list of new responsibilities and opportunities God brings into your life as you progress in recovery.

Blessings can be heavy, but they only become burdens when we hide the uncertainty or insecurity we feel.

Give thanks for these opportunities. Remember they are tokens of God's grace, not burdens. When they feel heavy, ask for help, and talk about this weight with a friend. Blessings can be heavy, but they only become burdens when we hide the uncertainty or insecurity we feel. This is a mark of maturity as we humbly depend on God and his people.

Remember that gaining freedom from addiction is not the end of your journey. Your addiction was sapping your energy to do things God called you to do, stealing the time in which you would do them, and undermining the confidence that God would bless your efforts. Be discerning about not overloading on these opportunities. But realize these opportunities to care for others are a significant part of becoming the person God created you to be (Matthew 22:27–40).

4. **Having answers instead of questions.** As you mature and receive new opportunities, you will likely be looked to for more answers. Your responses to the challenges of life are becoming grounded and hopeful, so people will want to know how you would approach their challenges. You begin to get the privilege of joining people at earlier stages in their journey of gaining freedom from addiction.

This is a time when pride can return in more subtle and socially acceptable ways. *We must never think that because a question is brought to us that we are the source of its answer.* We must never mistake the glory of the answer for the glory of the vessel that has been entrusted to carry that answer (2 Corinthians 4:7–18). We are merely the conduit of the hope and perspective that we have received from God and others in our journey of recovery.

- ▸ Allow the notes you've taken on your G4 journey to provide the hope and perspective you offer others to be rooted in the biblical truths that have undergirded your G4 journey.

Give yourself the freedom to be both excited and humble at the same time.

- ▸ **Read James 3:1–12.** Notice that James is writing to Christians coming out of a struggle (dispersion by religious persecution; see James 1:1) who are now rising to the position of teacher (3:1). He warns them about the temptation that comes with the increased power of their words in this new role. The message is that the awesome power of influence (James uses the imagery of bridles and fire) should keep us humble as we are coming into new positions of influence.

The changes we've discussed in this part of Step 8 are things we should be both excited about and cautious toward. We should be excited because they are indicators of God's grace at work in our life and producing growth. They are signs of maturation and progress. We should be cautious because they reveal the transition into new roles for which we will be less familiar. Give yourself the freedom to be both excited and humble at the same time.

## G4 GROUP DISCUSSION: STEP 8, PART TWO

As you discuss this material in G4 group, these questions are meant to facilitate a more honest and beneficial dialogue about this material. Anyone is free to respond to whichever questions they choose.

### Experienced Members

- How have/did you see temptation change for you as you entered Steps 7 and 8?
- What was the same and what needed to change in how you faced these temptations?

### New Members

- Does it encourage or discourage you to think about temptation mutating as you progress in recovery?
- How does seeing the emphasis on dependence later in the G4 journey help curb your instinct toward independence early in your process of recovery?
- How can we pray for you?

### Everyone

- Which of these four changes in temptation are most prevalent in your life and emotions?
- From the devotion on Galatians 2, what changes are you most prone to rebuild after tearing them down?
- Have you experienced a significant setback or victory since last meeting that you should tell the group?

# STEP 8
## PART THREE

### PREPARING FOR TRANSITION FROM G4

The video for this part of Step 8 can be found at: bradhambrick.com/addiction8p3.

This third part of Step 8 may feel like a change of pace. That is because it no longer has addiction as its primary focus. Instead, this section asks, "What should my life begin to look like as my addiction fades?" Again, we don't overcome addiction for the sake of overcoming addiction. We overcome addiction to live the life that God intended. This part of Step 8 is about laying the foundation to live wisely in your new freedom.

**Make sure you are in a small group.** *Trust takes time.* If you have been going through this material in a G4 group, the baton of trust will soon be passed to less recovery-focused relationships. One-way helping relationships (relationships with defined roles, like doctor–patient or counselor–counselee) are not healthy long-term as your primary source of support and encouragement. For a season or as a supplement to authentic peer-based friendships, these can be great. But long-term we need to learn to be honest with and gain support from two-way friendships. You also want to expand the focus of your spiritual maturity from just overcoming addiction to the full spectrum of character formation and discipleship.

The primary location in which this occurs is small groups. The name of these groups may vary from church to church: Sunday school, community groups, missional communities, etc. The point is you need to be in one and begin to participate in it in ways that are commensurate with how you've participated in G4. If you need help identifying which small group would be a good fit for you, talk with your pastor.

Some people object, "But these groups are shallower than G4. People in these groups aren't as serious about making significant changes in their life." That may be true. But that is why we say: *the church needs G4, and G4 needs the church.*

- *The church needs G4 because* there is great benefit to have subject-specific communities that are intensely focused on areas of needed change. It is hard for the general discipleship ministry of a church to do what G4 does. But the church also needs the model of G4's intentionality and vulnerability in its discipleship ministries to be examples of what it looks like to do in-depth sanctification work in highly authentic relationships.
- *G4 needs the church because* we need to avoid our struggle from becoming our identity, and we need to avoid reducing our spiritual maturity to how we're doing with a single struggle. You are more than your addiction. While God may have you remain in G4 as a leader, God intends to use you in ways that are outside G4. Those things God wants to do in and through you are meant to be done in concert with your local church.

> We don't overcome addiction for the sake of overcoming addiction. We overcome addiction to live the life that God intended.

The reason we emphasize becoming part of a small group now is that you don't need to graduate from G4 without having a community you're already established in. Your remaining time in Steps 8 and 9 should include meaningful engagement with a small group. You should not graduate G4 until this community is fulfilling the roles we are about to discuss.

**Learn accountability and encouragement on a broader scale.** Walking through this material with your G4 group may be the first time you have experienced ongoing, Christian accountability and encouragement. *Accountability is not just for life-dominating struggles. It is part of God's definition of healthy.* People who do not have relationships in which they are honest about their struggles while seeking accountability and encouragement are becoming unhealthy.

As you move from G4 to a general small group, you may wonder what accountability and encouragement will look like now. The seven points below are meant to guide you in the kind of relationships you are looking to form with your small group:

1. **Voluntary.** *Accountability is not something you have; it is something you do.* You must disclose what needs to be known to benefit from relationships. Hopefully, the experience you have had in G4 will encourage you to remain transparent and vulnerable.

2. **Trusted.** *The other person is someone you trust, admire their character, and believe has good judgment.* You are encouraged to join a small group now so that you can build this trust before graduating from G4.

3. **Mutual.** *Relationships that are one-sided tend to be short-lived.* In the small group, you will hear the weaknesses and struggles of others as you share your own. You will help carry their burdens as they help carry yours (Galatians 6:1–2).

4. **Scheduled.** *Accountability that is not scheduled tends to fade.* This is why small groups that meet on a weekly basis are an ideal place for accountability to occur. Everyone knows when to meet and has a shared expectation for how the accountability conversations will begin.

5. **Relational.** We want spiritual growth to become a lifestyle, not an event. This means that we invite accountability to be a part of our regular conversations, not just something that we do at a weekly meeting. *There should be times when we are doing accountability and don't realize it.* We're just being honest about what's hard.

6. **Comprehensive.** Accountability that exclusively fixates on one subject tends to become repetitive and fade. It also tends to reduce success to trusting God in a single area of life. *Good accountability calls us to become more like Christ in every facet of our life.*

7. **Encouraging.** Too often the word "accountability" carries the connotation of a sin hunt. When that is the case, accountability is only perceived to be working when it is negative. However, *accountability that lasts should celebrate growth in character as fervently as it works on slips in character.*

If you are looking for a tool to help develop these kinds of relationships in a small group that avoids making a discipleship environment overly therapeutic, consider *Transformative Friendships: Seven Questions to Deepen Any Relationship* in this Church-Based Counseling series.[1]

**Have a plan for future study.** A general rule of life is that we walk forward, but we drift backward. For some time now this G4 curriculum has provided intentional, structured processes for you to follow. If you leave that structure without a plan for continued growth, chances are, you will regress. Ephesians 5:15–16 calls us to intentionality, recognizing that time minus direction equals decay, not growth.

This entire study has been filled with devotional Bible studies. If you have not been taking the time to read the passages and reflect on the commentary and questions that accompany them, consider using those as a guide for daily Bible reading. This will be a way to reinforce your G4 journey and further solidify the biblical basis for what you've learned.

Step 7 in this curriculum referenced many resources that might be beneficial for you. If one of them stood out as significant, begin reading it as you complete Step 8 and begin forming a relationship of trust with a small group at your church. If none of these resources seemed like a good fit, then consider studying *Saints, Sufferers, and Sinners* by Michael Emlet[2] as a resource to help you solidify your progress.

**Make a formal transition plan.** As you prepare to graduate from G4, write out your transition plan.

- List the relationships and practices that need to be in place before you graduate.
- Consider any imminent, upcoming life events that would be better to navigate with the support of your G4 group.

- Write out a concise summary of the key truths and changes that have been most influential from your G4 journey. Share these with your small group.
- Write out your "yellow flags" (don't wait for the red ones) that are warning signs of relapse. Also, share these with your small group.

Review your plan with your G4 group. Get their input on what needs to be added to the plan. The graduation of a group member is an important event in the life of every member in the group. Honor the significance of your pending graduation by giving weight to the encouragement and concerns raised by your fellow G4 members.

A general rule of life is that we walk forward, but we drift backward.

Perseverance is boring and exciting at the same time. It is boring because change usually does not happen as fast in this phase. Early in recovery, change was bold and obvious. But change that is fast is often not as solid; it's more like a weed than a tree. Boring growth is solid growth. This is not meant to be pejorative. Satisfying growth is not boring, but it takes time. When you look back over a stretch of months or a year and think both, *Not much has changed*, and, *Life is good*, that is a momentous testimony to God's faithfulness and your perseverance. As that becomes your testimony, you are ready to enter Step 9.

► **Read Isaiah 61:1–4.** Begin by noticing that this passage celebrates people who are "oaks of righteousness" (v. 3). Oaks are strong trees that took the time to grow slow. That is what you've done to arrive at Step 8 in G4. Then notice that the people celebrated in this passage "proclaim liberty to captives" (v. 1). That is what your testimony has done at G4. Finally, notice that the people celebrated in this passage repaired "the ruined cities" (v. 4). As you continue to cultivate a fruitful life from what addiction destroyed, that is the work you will continue long after you graduate from G4.

## G4 GROUP DISCUSSION: STEP 8, PART THREE

As you discuss this material in G4 group, these questions are meant to facilitate a more honest and beneficial dialogue about this material. Anyone is free to respond to whichever questions they choose.

### Experienced Members

- How has your time in G4 enriched your Christian relationships outside G4?
- What have you learned from seeing other members graduate from G4?

### New Members

- What encouragement do you take from the fact that G4 is designed for you to graduate from it?
- Even earlier in your G4 journey, how have you been challenged by the idea, "we walk forward, but we drift backward"?
- How can we pray for you?

### Everyone

- In your own words, summarize what is meant by "The church needs G4, and G4 needs the church."
- In your own words, summarize what is meant by "Perseverance is boring and exciting at the same time."
- Have you experienced a significant setback or victory since last meeting that you should tell the group?

Living Free to Enjoy the Life God Intended

---

# STEP 9

## STEWARD all of my life for God's glory.

---

At the end of this step, I want to be able to say . . .

**"God has been faithful in my battle against addiction.**
**I am learning what it means to live out of my new identity in Christ.**
**God's faithfulness has pushed me to ask the question, 'How can I be a conduit of his grace to others?'**
**As I have sought God, examined my life, and consulted with fellow believers,**
**I believe this is what it looks like for me to steward God's grace now [describe]."**

# STEP 9

## PART ONE

### NINE QUESTIONS TO STEWARD YOUR LIFE FOR GOD'S GLORY

The video for this part of Step 9 can be found at: bradhambrick.com/addiction9p1.

If the law of God can be summarized in a positive command (Matthew 22:37–40), then we must end this study talking about how to run to God rather than merely how to run from addiction. *Life is not about what we avoid, but what we pursue.* How we run to God's design for our life finds a unique expression in each person's life. For this reason, you will do most of the writing in this step. We will simply provide you with the questions to consider.

The goal is to find things that you could give yourself to more passionately than you once gave yourself to your addiction. Not just temporal, slightly healthier things, but eternally significant things that create a sense of purpose and keep you connected with a community of faith as you continue to grow toward Christlikeness. Even secular counselors recognize the need for this kind of purpose to live free from addiction.

> The absence of the addictive behavior is not sufficient to successfully maintain the change and become an ex-addict. In order to sustain recovery, new behaviors and reinforcing experiences must become part of a new way of living in the world . . . Taking away an addiction leaves a void that must be filled by alternative satisfying reinforcers for the economics of recovery to work. —Carlo DiClemente[1]

- **Read Luke 11:24–26.** This is a terrifying warning about removing sin without also replacing it with God's purposes for your life. When we replace sin with a "God-ignoring healthy life" (a contradiction) we become proud and defensive regarding further change. Our idols (Step 3) become more functional, so the warning system of adverse consequences is muted. Then, when our idols cease to satisfy and become disruptive again (as they inevitably will), we are less likely to return to God, the Bible, and the gospel because they didn't really work the first time. Indeed, "the last state of that person is worse than the first" (v. 26). This is why Step 9 is essential for ongoing victory over addiction.

The goal is to find things that you could give yourself to more passionately than you once gave yourself to your addiction.

- **Read Ephesians 2:8–10.** In G4 we have traveled through the gospel (vv. 8–9) to good works (v. 10). *The nine steps are merely the gospel in slow motion.* We are not now exiting the gospel to do good works but cultivating the fruit of the gospel. Paul says that there are good works that God has prepared for every believer and that these should define our daily lives ("that we should walk in them" [v. 10]). This should give you hope that there are answers to the questions you will be asked in Step 9. You can have the confidence that comes from the promises of Scripture that God has a design for your life and wants you to know what it is.

As you read through and answer these **nine questions**, remember God's patience and timing. There will be some aspects of God's design that you can engage immediately. But there will also be ways you want to serve God that will require you to mature more or be equipped before you are prepared to fulfill them. The main thing is to begin to have a vision for life that involves being God's servant and actively engaging that vision where you are currently equipped.

1. **Am I willing to commit my life to whatever God asks of me?** This is a "do not pass go" question. If your answer is no, it will bias the answers you give to each subsequent question. Do not get lost in guilt or pretend that your answer is yes (both

responses would lead you back into an addictive lifestyle). Rather, identify the obstacle. What is the cost you are unwilling to pay? Put it into words. Wrestle with what it means to trust God with this part of your life too.

Are there specific things you believe God is asking of you? Be sure to record your thoughts on this question before reflecting on the subsequent questions.

2. **What roles have I neglected that God has placed me in?** The first part of being a good steward of one's life is to fulfill one's primary roles with excellence. When Paul says in Ephesians 5:17 that we are to "understand what the will of the Lord is," he goes on to describe God's design for major life roles (spouse, parent, child, and worker in 5:22–6:9).

3. **What are my spiritual gifts?** Stewarding your life for the glory of God involves utilizing the spiritual gifts God has given you. God gives spiritual gifts that coincide with the calling he places on every believer's life. Read Romans 12:1–8 and 1 Corinthians 12:1–30. If you need further assistance discerning this, talk to a pastor about taking a spiritual gifts inventory.

4. **For what group of people (age, struggle, career, ethnicity, etc.) am I burdened?** From God's earliest covenant with people, his intention was to bless us that we might be a blessing to others (Genesis 12:2). Investing your life in those you have a burden for allows you to be others-minded and find joy in it.

5. **What am I passionate about?** At this point in the stewardship evaluation, you can begin to see Psalm 37:3–8 fulfilled in your life. What are the God-exalting "delights" in your life (v. 4)? What wholesome things can you give yourself to and you are more energized afterward than before you started?

6. **With what talents or abilities has God blessed me?** These don't have to be spiritual gifts. Read the amazing description of abilities God gave Bezalel and how he used those abilities to serve God (Exodus 31:1–11). Think through the skills and expertise you have accumulated in your life.

7. **What are my unique life experiences?** Both pleasant and unpleasant experiences should be listed. We are sometimes tempted to think that God can only use the good or spiritual experiences of our lives. God is glad to use our successes (Matthew 5:16), but God also delights in displaying his grace by transforming our low points for his glory (2 Corinthians 1:3–5).

8. **Where do my talents and passions match up with the needs in my church and community?** We should seek to steward our lives in cooperation with our local church. God's way of blessing and maturing those we serve is through the body of Christ, the church. By identifying where your gifts, burdens, passions, and abilities fit within (or expand) your church's ministries, you are maximizing the impact that service can have on those you are seeking to bless.

9. **How would God have me bring these things together to glorify him?** This is not a new question, but a summary question. Look back over what you have written. Talk about it with your Christian friends, family, mentor, or pastors. Dedicate a time to prayerfully ask God to give you a sense of direction. Then begin serving as a way to steward your life for God's glory.

"Blessed are those who hunger and thirst for righteousness,
for they shall be satisfied." —Matthew 5:6

## G4 GROUP DISCUSSION: STEP 9, PART ONE

As you discuss this material in G4 group, these questions are meant to facilitate a more honest and beneficial dialogue about this material. Anyone is free to respond to whichever questions they choose.

### Experienced Members

- As you reflected on these questions, what do you believe is God's purpose for you in this next season of life?
- Which of these questions was most influential for you in discerning what God has for you next?

### New Members

- Does talking about Step 9 create a sense of wanting to rush your journey?
- How does seeing the culmination of your G4 journey create hope and motivation for you?
- How can we pray for you?

### Everyone

- Can you go through the nine steps and articulate how "the nine steps are merely the gospel in slow motion"?
- Based on the devotional from Luke 11, what cautions do you take for your journey in recovery?
- Have you experienced a significant setback or victory since last meeting that you should tell the group?

## APPENDIX A

# A Word to G4 Group Leaders

Thank you for your willingness to lead a G4 group! This postscript is a microcosm of *Facilitating Church-Based Counseling Groups: A Leader's Guide for Group-Based Counseling Ministry* (New Growth, 2023), the leader's guide for G4 series books. The points below are explained and illustrated in greater detail in that resource. If you have already read *Facilitating*, this postscript is your cheat sheet reminder page. If you have not yet read *Facilitating*, then this is your "sampler's platter" to entice you to take the next step in training as a counseling group leader.

Here are a few things you need to know about leading a G4 group:

- G4 series curriculums facilitate an **open group model**—meaning anyone can join the group at any time and everyone present is likely to be at a different place on their journey.
- Because G4 is an open group model, your role is *not* to serve as a counselor for each person in the group; instead, you are a **facilitator of the group**.
- As the group facilitator, your two primary tasks are to **lead the discussion** each evening and **manage the morale** of the group.
- The **video teaching** for each segment of this journey is meant to alleviate the pressure for you to feel like a subject matter expert. For this curriculum, the video teaching can be found at **bradhambrick.com/addiction**. The QR code at the beginning of each new section will take participants to the video clip for that section.
- The **expectation for each participant** of the group is to: (a) faithfully attend G4, (b) watch the video clip for the section

they are working on, (c) read, reflect, and complete exercises for that section, and (d) come ready to discuss the progress or challenges they faced that week. Since everyone works at their own pace, you're not assessing the pace of their journey, simply their commitment to move forward.

- Counseling groups, like G4, are for those who are **ready to change** or strongly considering their need for change. It is not your role or the role of the group to convince people to take steps they are unwilling to take. The group exists to support, not convince.
- Each **G4 curriculum is intentionally long.** No one should finish nine steps in nine weeks. While that might give you a good education about addition, it is not sufficient time to cement change over a life-dominating struggle. In reality, your group or a participant may not finish one part of each step each week. G4 is less about education (mastering content) and more about transformation (accomplishing change). That takes time. G4 is not a race. No prizes are given for finishing first or fast. The reward of a restored life is the fruit of finishing well.
- As you can begin to see, G4 is a **place of support with a curriculum that provides guidance**. As you think of G4, those should be your two guiding principles. First, lead the group in a way that it becomes a place of mutual support. Second, allow the curriculum to provide counsel. The sharing time in a group is when these two components come together as members hear stories of how the curriculum was applied in each other's lives.
- When **someone needs more help than G4 can provide**, help them find a resource in your community that provides that care and continue, if they are willing, to provide the support of your G4 group. You are not failing if someone needs more than your G4 group can provide. Do what you can do well, and point people to additional resources. In most cases, those additional resources will be more effective because of the support of G4. You will notice that there are not a lot of "stories" in G4 curriculum. That is because the testimony of fellow G4 participants are the most powerful illustrations.

- To accomplish these objectives, we **recommend a schedule** for a G4 group that follows the outline below. Each segment is defined and illustrated in greater depth in *Facilitating Church-Based Counseling Groups.*
    - » Welcome and orient new guests.
    - » Personal updates (5–10 minutes).
    - » Facilitating and sharing (30–40 minutes). These are often done simultaneously or in either order. You are free to lead your group in the way that serves it best.
        - Covering a step or step segment (10–15 minutes).
        - Personal step work progress and accountability (20–25 minutes).
    - » Prayer (5–10 minutes).

Serve your group with these general parameters in mind. Don't underestimate the value of having a weekly place to meet, discuss, and receive encouragement for a shared life struggle. Life-dominating struggles make us feel alone, like no one else could understand. Your group is an oasis that dispels this lie. As the leader, you are the person holding out the hope that, while we may not see the change we desire week-to-week, when we look at the lives of faithful participants month-to-month, we are encouraged by God's faithfulness. As we look at the legacy of a group year-to-year, we move from encouragement to amazement at what God accomplishes.

G4 is a long-game ministry. Stay the course, be faithful in your role, encourage participants to persevere in the process, and you will see lives transformed by the gospel in ways that sustain your soul in this weighty ministry!

## APPENDIX B

# How to Conduct an Effective Intervention

If you are reading this appendix, you are *hurting* because someone you love is destroying their life with drugs and alcohol. You likely feel *angry* that they cannot see what they are doing to themselves and others. You feel *frustrated* that previous conversations have not been heard. Part of you wants to give up and part of you refuses to do so. Often, we come to the idea of conducting an intervention as a last-ditch effort to get through to someone that we love. This appendix is meant to help you take this step strategically rather than desperately.

We need to model the courage it will take to acknowledge an addiction in the way we address the addiction.

Sometimes we are prone to think that interventions are a modern invention, but intentional, tough love conversations with someone we know who is spiraling in their self-destructive choices have always been part of God's design.

> Curiously, intervention is hailed as one of the most significant advances in drug treatment. Yet church discipline is the original and intervention the imitator. —Ed Welch[1]

If you read **Matthew 18:15–20**, the primary biblical passage for outlining the process of church discipline, you see an intentional order: personal conversation, small group conversation, and large group conversation. This raises an **important question** as you consider conducting an intervention: Have you had a direct personal conversation that addresses your concerns?

A group intervention should not be the first attempt to address an addiction. We need to model the courage it will take to acknowledge an addiction in the way we address the addiction. That entails having the courage to say, "I am concerned about you, and I can't be your friend and be silent. I think you have a problem with [substance]. Can we talk about it?"

Nobody with a substance abuse problem ever wants to hear the phrase, "You have a problem." In fact, most people in the midst of addiction refuse to think they have a problem at all. They are apt to deny it—strongly. But the reality is that hearing a friend or loved one utter those four simple words may save someone's life.

*A group intervention is most effective when it's the culmination and echo of these loving, personal interventions.* With that said, let's look at how to conduct an effective group intervention in three phases.

## PHASE ONE: BEFORE THE INTERVENTION

An effective intervention is not a spontaneous event. It requires planning and preparation. Each of the factors below is an important part of preparing for an effective intervention.

- **Pray.** *You desire an outcome that is more than you are able to accomplish even if you do everything in your power as well as you possibly can.* You can't force your friend's eyes open to the destructiveness of their choices. You want humility to replace defensiveness. You want acknowledgment to replace denial. Those are not things we can manufacture. Those are changes only God can create in the heart of your friend.

  When we fail to recognize this, we either become controlling or codependent; we either try to force change or blame ourselves if our friend doesn't begin to pursue recovery. For these reasons, we need to pray (protecting our own heart) as much as our friend needs to be prayed for (that God would soften their heart).
- **Decide who.** Three questions should determine who participates in the intervention. An ideal number for an intervention is 5–10 people. Preferably these people would represent different spheres of the individual's life (i.e., family, work, church, friends, etc.).

1. *Who has the quality of relationship to allow their voice to be heard?* It should be obvious why each person present has a vested interest in the individual acknowledging their addiction. It doesn't make sense to have a stranger at an intervention.
2. *Who has the concrete information that is most irrefutable?* More will be said about being concrete in a latter point.
3. *Who has sufficient self-control to ensure their presence will not become a distraction?* Immature or emotionally reactive members of the intervention team can easily derail the purpose of the meeting.

- **Decide when and where.** There is no such thing as a perfect moment, however, giving thought to when and where an intervention takes place can increase the meeting's opportunity to be successful. An intervention should not occur in a public place (i.e., restaurant, work office, etc.). Embarrassment would distract from the content of the meeting.

  Most often interventions are staged events, meaning the individual being confronted is unaware the meeting will occur. Usually this involves having the intervention team present at the individual's home or apartment at a time when he/she will be predictably arriving (i.e., after work or class). Another possibility is having someone—perhaps the parents—invite the individual to their home and have the intervention team present when he/she arrives.
- **Decide how.** An intervention should not be a long meeting because its effectiveness is not found in the abundance of words. *The meeting needs to stay on message*, and unless you prepare and rehearse for the meeting, that is unlikely to occur. It is recommended that you have a written agenda for the meeting. It should be simple enough that those on the intervention team don't need to have it in their hand. A sample meeting plan might look like this:

  *Note:* Each person who speaks should begin by expressing their love for the individual and saying that their goal is to see them restored to health, not to punish or shame them. The leader will likely call on each person when it is their turn to speak.

- » **Leader:** Express love for the person, explain reason for meeting, and ask for cooperation with the meeting.
  - Reason for the meeting: "We believe you have a problem and cannot in good conscience remain silent."
  - Process for the meeting: "We want you to hear us, and after that, we're committed to hearing you."
- » **Participant One:** Express love for the person and cite most concrete examples of *risk-taking behaviors* (i.e., drinking and driving, having to pay back a threatening drug dealer, etc.).
- » **Participant Two:** Express love for the person and cite most concrete examples of *health deterioration* (i.e., see Step 2 material).
- » **Participant Three:** Express love for the person and cite most concrete examples of *neglecting relationships that the individual is known to value* (i.e., lack of time with children, lying, neglecting friends, etc.).
- » **Participant Four:** Express love for the person and cite most concrete examples of *financial deterioration* (i.e., borrowing money, being behind on bills, etc.).
- » **Participant Five:** Express love for the person and cite most concrete examples of *neglecting school or work* (i.e., negative performance evaluations, examples of being fired, dropping grades, etc.).
  - Each person present should speak to an aspect of how the individual's addiction is destroying their quality of life. Only the most irrefutable areas of life and examples should be used.
- » **Leader:** "In light of these concerns and our love for you, we believe you need to seek help for your addiction. We have several options we believe are viable and effective. We are asking that you consider these [describe]."
- » **Listen:** "We know what we've said cannot be easy to hear, but we want to know what you think and what you think would be wise for you to do in light of the concerns we've raised."
- » If the intervention is rejected, meaning the individual is unwilling to acknowledge the addiction and seek help, then

the meeting would conclude with a list of consequences the group is willing to mutually enforce for the individual's good.
  - » If the intervention is embraced, then the group becomes a support network for the individual as he/she begins to enact the steps agreed upon and work on a more comprehensive plan of recovery.
- **Be concrete.** *Every example you use should be factual and irrefutable.* Expect that the weakest example you verbalize in the intervention will be the focal point for the individual's response. Do not provide a weak example that could be used to discredit the other concerns. Step 2 of this material will help you think through the most concrete examples.

> The goal of an intervention is not acknowledgment but action.

- **Repent personally.** It is easy for the level of frustration and hurt amongst the intervention team to overpower their sense of empathy. When this happens, the intervention will feel harsh and unloving. Amongst each other, the intervention team should spend some time acknowledging their personal need for the same grace that they want their friend to embrace.

  This exercise generates a better appreciation for the degree of vulnerability that the group is asking their friend to display. While this exercise is unlikely to change the content of what is shared or asked (nor should it), it is very likely to impact the tone of the meeting.
- **Rehearse.** If the time from initiating the meeting to listening is going to be less than thirty minutes (which is ideal), then each person will need to think through what they are going to say and practice saying it. Just like it takes longer to write a short email than a long one, it takes a bit of work to concisely say important things.

  As the intervention team rehearses the meeting, several questions need to be asked about each segment of the meeting:
  - » Is it clear that love for the individual is more important than the pain they've caused or the damage they've done?

  - Are any examples used that sound weak or could be easily debunked?
  - Is language used that begins to make excuses for or explains away addictive behavior?

At the end of rehearsing for the meeting, it is wise to role-play how the individual might respond so that the group can think through how to end the meeting in each instance. Possible responses to prepare for would include the following:

  - Active Resistance: "You're all wrong. I don't have a problem."
  - Being Personally Offended: "I can't believe you would all team up and attack me this way."
  - Debating Details: "I can explain why every example you've given isn't as bad as you say."
  - Changing Who's on Trial: "How can you say this about me when you [blank]?"
  - Passive Compliance: "You've given me some things I need to think about, and I'll think about what you've said."
  - Getting Lost in Sorrow: "[Sobbing] I can't believe I've been as bad as you say. I'm a horrible person/friend."
  - Active Repentance: "I do have a problem. I need to address it. [Blank] option seems like the best start." This is the response you are praying for—where your friend engages one of the options the team proposed.
  - Other: You know your friend. What other responses seem likely?

- **Research options.** The goal of an intervention is not acknowledgment but action; acknowledgment is merely a means to an end. The team needs to have tangible, actionable follow-up steps to begin the process of recovery, which can be engaged immediately following the meeting.
  - If the substance abused and degree of abuse warrant detox, then the intervention team needs to know the local detox centers and entry process. This can be determined by calling the local hospitals.
  - Know the days and times of local recovery group meetings or ministries. Timing the intervention to occur just before one of these meetings would be ideal.

» Know the intake process for viable residential programs if this is a potential good fit for your friend.

» Have a list of local counselors who specialize in addiction assessment and counseling. If this seems to be the most agreeable next step, ask the counselor if you can scholarship a session immediately following the intervention.

  - *Note:* The individual would have to make the appointment and complete the necessary paperwork. But having a scheduled, paid assessment session already in place can help remove barriers from taking immediate action.

> Your goal is to prompt your loved one to engage in the recovery process.

Remember, don't offer options that aren't a good fit. The type of resources in your community or the type of addiction your friend struggles with should determine your recommendations. Providing bad follow-up options will undermine an otherwise well-run intervention.

You'll notice an effective intervention is preceded by many phone calls and, potentially, some financial investment. It is worth it. In an intervention, you are likely risking your last remaining social capital. The work leading into an intervention helps make sure this risk is a good investment.

From this research, you will be able to use names when referencing options (i.e., "When we spoke to Dr. Smith at the detox center, she said . . . And counselor Davis indicated his initial assessment helps individuals determine . . ."). Being able to talk about this concretely helps make everything you say seem more immediately actionable and reasonable.

## PHASE TWO: DURING THE INTERVENTION

*Once you get to the intervention, the only surprises should be whether your friend shows up and how he/she responds at the end.* If you prepare well, everything in the middle should be well established. Here are some suggestions for the intervention:

- **Remember the objective.** Your goal is to prompt your loved one to engage in the recovery process. When you begin to think your goal is to save your loved one, the dynamics of the meeting will become much more emotionally intense. Review the meeting objective with the intervention team prior to the meeting.
- **Never meet resistance head-on.** *If the intervention becomes an argument or debate, you lose*; the likelihood your friend will engage recovery diminishes significantly. The following points are meant to help you roll with the resistance that is likely in the intervention without delving into debate or conceding to your friend's perspective.[2]
    - » *Stay emotionally even-keeled.* When you display anger or exasperation, you become a distraction to your point. Your friend can focus on how you're talking instead of what you're saying. Being at peace with the idea that you can't change anyone and that your responsibility is to speak the truth in love (i.e., the most receivable manner under the circumstances) will help you remain even-keeled.
    - » *Evidence good listening.* At the beginning of the meeting, you said you would listen. So, listen. If your friend begins to talk for a long time and doesn't want to be interrupted, ask if you can take notes because what they're saying is important to you. Begin what you say, when it's your turn to speak, with a summary of what they've said, not a rebuttal. Represent the tone and content of their words fairly when you summarize.
    - » *Raise discrepancies as friendly questions.* After you summarize, there will doubtless be discrepancies in what they've said. It is okay to point these out. Be sure you begin with the most central and solid examples. Be sure you raise the discrepancy with respect.

      You might say, "You say you want to be a good husband and father, but your wife says you are usually home for less than an hour before you start drinking each evening. How does that fit with your desire to have a strong family?" or, "You say your career is important to you, but your last three performance reviews have marked you down for inability to focus at work because of sleepiness and excessive sick days when you're hungover. We have a hard time understanding how your lifestyle is fitting with your life goals." After a statement like this, listen again.

> If there is going to be a battle, you want it to be between the person and God, not between the person and yourself. . . . If love rather than anger is clearly expressed during the intervention, addicts typically appreciate what was done after they are sober. —Ed Welch[3]

> The most important post-intervention note is to follow through on whatever is decided at the intervention.

» *Ask how they would like the concern raised.* If raising discrepancies meets resistance, don't meet that resistance head-on either. You might say something like this, "We know these things are hard to hear. We love you too much to be silent. Can you tell us how to raise these concerns in a way that is more receivable? We have tried as individuals, but we didn't feel heard. We are open to anything that is truly for your good." Then, listen.

» *Respect their right to choose.* Your friend's choice to accept or reject the invitation to engage in recovery will come at the end of the meeting—for better or worse. The team needs to be prepared for either outcome and should resist looping the meeting back to the beginning when the desired outcome is not met. If your friend chooses to dismiss the concerns raised, then the next point becomes relevant.

- **Provide consequences.** Consequences are not the same as punishments. *Punishments seek to inflict unpleasant experiences to coerce or motivate change. Consequences, in this context, are a way for those near an addict to opt out of supporting or enabling the addictive lifestyle.*

> Families often give enough financial and personal support for the Precontemplator to avoid the harshest of consequences of their addiction. In effect, these

families neutralize the educational effects of negative consequences. —Carlo DiClemente[4]

Consequences might include:

- » Cutting off or restricting access to the money necessary to support the addiction.
- » Reporting an instance of suspected DUI activity to law enforcement.
- » Having a set time at which doors will be locked and access to the home will be unavailable until the morning.
- » Limiting access to children to supervised times when sobriety can be verified.
  - ▪ Note: this step would require some legal intervention to be enforceable if they are uncooperative.
- » Asking them to move out of the home and forcing them to bear the responsibilities of living independently.
- » Refusing to rescue the individual from the consequences (direct or indirect) related to their addictive lifestyle.

## PHASE THREE: AFTER THE INTERVENTION

The most important post-intervention note is to follow through on whatever is decided at the intervention. If your friend is cooperative, follow through on the support roles you indicated you would play. If your friend is uncooperative, follow through on the consequences you indicated you would enforce.

In many ways this is the hardest part of the intervention. This difficulty is why the group intervention is good for each member of the intervention team. *The group provides accountability for each member of the group whether it is to fulfill supportive roles or to avoid circumventing consequences.* When there is cooperation, the group also allows the supportive roles to be divided amongst more people so that the level of support can be sustained over an extended period of time, because recovery is usually an extended process.

If you or one of the intervention team members struggle to consistently follow through on the outcomes arrived at in the intervention (support in recovery or consequences for resisting recovery), then it is recommended you utilize the resource at bradhambrick.com/care teams05 to enhance the aftercare aspect of the intervention.

# Notes

**Step 1; Part One**

1. Carlo DiClemente, *Addictions and Change* (New York: Guilford Press, 2003), 144.

2. From the testimony of the cofounder of Celebrate Recovery, John Baker, *Celebrate Recovery: Leader's Guide* (Nashville: Harper Christian Resources, 2016), 15.

**Step 1; Part Two**

1. Craig Nakken, *The Addictive Personality* (Center City, MN: Hazelden Publishing, 1996).

2. Ed Welch, *Addictions: A Banquet in the Grave* (Phillipsburg, NJ: P&R, 2001).

3. Carlo DiClemente, *Addictions and Change* (New York: Guilford Press, 2003), 50, 52.

4. Welch, *Addictions*, 35.

5. DiClemente, *Addictions and Change*, 4.

6. Gerald May, *Addictions and Grace* (New York: HarperOne, 2007), 24, 33.

7. Nakken, *The Addictive Personality*, 10.

8. Nakken, *The Addictive Personality,* 113.

9. Kent Dunnington, *Addiction and Virtue: Beyond the Models of Disease and Choice* (Westmont, IL: IVP Academic, 2011), 129.

10. Louis Berkhof, *Systematic Theology: New Combined Edition* (Grand Rapids: Eerdmans, 1996), 227, 233.

11. Linda Mercadante, *Victims and Sinners* (Louisville, KY: Westminster John Knox Press, 1996), 110.

**Step 1; Part Three**

1. Ed Welch, *Crossroads: A Step-by-Step Guide Away from Addiction* (Greensboro, NC: New Growth, 2008), 33, 36.

2. John Baker, *Celebrate Recovery: Leader's Guide* (Nashville: Harper Christian Resources, 2016), 59, 60, 79.

3. Gerald May, *Addictions and Grace* (New York: HarperOne, 2007), 179.

4. If you are not aware of a local G4 group, information for finding a counselor or support group to help you in your journey can be found at bradhambrick.com/findacounselor.

5. Welch, *Crossroads*, 3.

6. Bill Wilson, *Alcoholics Anonymous: The Big Book Fourth Edition* (New York: Alcoholics Anonymous World Services, 2001, original 1939), 13.

**Step 2; Part One**

1. Carlo DiClemente, *Addictions and Change* (New York: Guilford Press, 2003), 91.

**Step 2; Part Two**

1. Marc Schuckit, *Drug and Alcohol Abuse: A Clinical Guide to Diagnosis and Treatment* (New York: Springer, 2005), 74.

2. Cornelius Plantinga, Jr, *Not the Way It's Supposed to Be: A Breviary of Sin* (Grand Rapids: Eerdmans, 1996), 131.

3. Paul Tripp, *Instruments in the Redeemer's Hand* (Phillipsburg, NJ: P&R, 2002), 260.

**Step 2; Part Three**

1. Ed Welch, *Crossroads: A Step-by-Step Guide Away from Addiction* (Greensboro, NC: New Growth, 2008), 25.

2. Adapted from William Miller et al., *Motivational Enhancement Therapy Manual* (Rockville, MD: Echo Point Books, 1999), 34–39. Used by permission.

3. Welch, *Crossroads*, 3, 92.

4. Carlo DiClemente, *Addictions and Change* (New York: Guilford Press, 2003), 28.

**Step 3; Part Two**

1. Ed Welch, *Crossroads: A Step-by-Step Guide Away from Addiction* (Greensboro, NC: New Growth, 2008), 14.

2. Kent Dunnington, *Addiction and Virtue: Beyond the Models of Disease and Choice* (Westmont, IL: IVP Academic, 2011), 153.

**Step 4; Part One**

1. Gerald May, *Addictions and Grace* (New York: HarperOne, 2007), 122.

2. A. W. Tozer, *The Knowledge of the Holy* (Independent Publishing Platform, 2017), 1.

3. Ed Welch, *Addictions: A Banquet in the Grave* (Phillipsburg, NJ: P&R, 2001), 213.

**Step 4; Part Two**

1. John Baker, *Celebrate Recovery: Leader's Guide* (Nashville: Harper Christian Resources, 2016), 16.

**Step 5; Part Two**

1. These points were adapted from the excellent work on confession by Ken Sande in *Peacemaking for Families* (Colorado Springs: Focus on the Family, 2002). I highly commend this book as you are seeking to restore health in your relationships with family and friends.

**Step 5; Part Three**

1. John Baker, *Celebrate Recovery: Leader's Guide* (Nashville: Harper Christian Resources, 2016), 162.

**Step 6; Part One**

1. Kent Dunnington, *Addiction and Virtue: Beyond the Models of Disease and Choice* (Westmont, IL: IVP Academic, 2011), 185.

**Step 6; Part Two**

1. This line is frequently used by and borrowed from Paul Tripp.

2. Carlo DiClemente, *Addictions and Change* (New York: Guilford Press, 2003), 13.

**Step 6; Part Three**

1. John Baker, *Celebrate Recovery: Leader's Guide* (Nashville: Harper Christian Resources, 2016), 56.

**Step 6; Part Five**

1. Ed Welch, *Addictions: A Banquet in the Grave* (Phillipsburg, NJ: P&R, 2001), 142.

2. Kent Dunnington, *Addiction and Virtue: Beyond the Models of Disease and Choice* (Westmont, IL: IVP Academic, 2011), 178.

3. Dunnington, *Addiction and Virtue*, 176.

**Step 7; Part One**

1. These four phases of relapse are adapted from Stephen Arterburn and Linda Mintle's categories of complacency, confusion, compromise, catastrophe in *Lose It for Life* (Nashville: Thomas Nelson, 2011), 228–30.

**Step 7; Part Two**

1. David Powlison, *Sexual Addiction: Freedom from Compulsive Behavior* (Greensboro, NC: New Growth, 2010), 8–10.

**Step 7; Part Three**

1. Ed Welch, *Addictions: A Banquet in the Grave* (Phillipsburg, NJ: P&R, 2001), 124.

2. Carlo DiClemente, *Addictions and Change* (New York: Guilford Press, 2003), 195.

**Step 8; Part One**

1. C. S. Lewis, *Mere Christianity* (New York: Harper San Francisco, 1980), 142.

**Step 8; Part Three**

1. Brad Hambrick, *Transformative Friendships: Seven Questions to Deepen Any Relationship* (Greensboro, NC: New Growth Press, 2024).

2. Michael Emlet, *Saints, Sufferers, and Sinners: Loving Others as God Loves Us* (Greensboro, NC: New Growth Press, 2021).

**Step 9; Part One**

1. Carlo DiClemente, *Addictions and Change* (New York: Guilford Press, 2003), 190, 193.

**Appendix B**

1. Ed Welch, *Addictions: A Banquet in the Grave* (Phillipsburg, NJ: P&R, 2001), 96.

2. Additional guidance on the concept of "rolling with resistance" can be found at bradhambrick.com/resistance.

3. Welch, *Addictions*, 94, 110.

4. Carlo DiClemente, *Addictions and Change* (New York: Guilford Press, 2003), 123.